ENGLISH G

| G9 |

# access 6

## WORKBOOK



Deine **interaktiven Gratis-Übungen**, **Audios** und **Erklärfilme** findest du auf scook.de. Dort gibst du den unten stehenden Zugangscode in die Box ein.

Dein Zugangscode auf
www.scook.de | genuwe

Cornelsen

# Who are you?

1

2

## 1 Profile photos

➜ SB (pp. 10–11) • Wordbank 1

In your exercise book, describe the people in the profile photos. How do you think they want others to see them? Which person would you prefer to be friends with, and why?

- *Photo 1 shows ...*
- *He is dressed ...*
- *Photo 2 looks as if it was taken ...*
- *I think I would prefer to be friends with ...*
- *The boy in photo 1 looks more ... than the girl in photo 2 ... because ...*

## 2 What does your profile photo say about you?

➜ SB (p. 11) • SMC 26 (p. 71)

a) You are going to listen to an interview with a social media expert about profile photos. Read the sentences in b) first. Then guess how the sentences might continue. Write in your exercise book.

b) 01 Complete the sentences while you listen. Compare the full sentences you wrote in your exercise book with Nisha's answers. Did you manage to guess any of them correctly?

1 Profile photos have been studied in recent years because increased online communication ____________

______________________________

2 Nisha thinks that deciding quickly what someone is like is ____________

______________________________

3 If someone isn't close to the camera, it can mean they ____________

______________________________

4 Steve's creative profile photos suggest that he is ____________

______________________________

5 In Nisha's opinion, young people use group photos because it can ____________

______________________________

6 Three reasons why people might use a baby photo for their profile photo are: (1) they don't want to grow up,

(2) they think ____________

## 3 Poems about identity ➜ SB (pp. 12–14)

a) Read the two poems. How do they explore the theme of identity? Write about 100 words in your exercise book.

*Poem 1 is about how someone's identity can be linked to ...*

### Accent

*As soon as he opens his mouth, his city appears,*
*Written in giant neon[1] letters across his forehead[2].*
*His accent was made in Liverpool's melting pot[3]:*
*a spoonful[4] of Lancashire[5], a dollop[6] of Irish,*
*and a pinch[7] of Welsh –*
*all seasoned[8] with a sprinkle[9] of Scandinavian[10].*
*Down south, they hear it*
*And straight away they think they know him.*
*He must have football in his blood*
*(whether it's red or blue),*
*a spirit[11] as tough as old boots*
*and a cheeky[12] sense of humour.*
*Just for a change,*
*he'd love someone to ask him*
*who he really is.*

### Genetics[13]

*I was born with Mom's big brown eyes.*
*"She's her mother's daughter," they said.*
*My father gave me my eyebrows[14] – two straight brush strokes[15] –*
*And a frown that could start World War Three.*
*My teeth came through crooked[16], like broken piano keys*
*And everybody said I had Aunt Julia's smile.*
*They all predicted[17]*
*That I would have straight, silky hair,*
*Dark as molasses[18], like Grandpa's. Like everyone's.*
*But it came through rough and curly*
*And dark red, like rust[19].*
*It's a wild beast[20] that will not be tamed[21].*
*But I love it.*
*It's the only part of me that's really mine.*

b) ● Choose three short phrases from each poem that speak to your emotions. In your exercise book, explain why you find them moving.

*I think that "giant neon letters" (Accent, l.2) is a good way to explain how ... "He must have football in his blood" (l.9) – this is a strong image that shows how ... "like broken piano keys" (Genetics, l.5) – this image is good because piano keys are ... "a wild beast" (l.12) – this is a funny way to describe ...*

c) Share your answers to a) and b) with a partner.

d) For each poem, choose a phrase that you found difficult to understand. What do you think it could mean? Discuss your ideas with your partner.

*In the first poem, I'm not sure about the meaning of ... It could be ... What do you think?*

## 4 Talking about imagery ➜ SB (p. 15)

a) ○ Underline the correct answer.

1 **Similes and metaphors:** cannot be combined in one image / are two common ways of creating images in the readers' minds / compare things using *as* or *like*.
2 **Metaphors:** are usually thought to be stronger than similes / are easy to recognize because they always use the verb to be / don't work in the same sentence as similes.
3 **Similes:** are always used before metaphors / often describe someone's character or appearance / suggest that one thing is another thing.

b) Go back to the poems in exercise 3. In each poem, underline at least three similes and three metaphors in different colours. Check your answers with a partner.

c) Choose one example of imagery from each poem and say why you like it/don't like it. Share your answers with a partner.

*In poem 1, I like the metaphor of the person with neon letters on his head ...*
*I think it's a good way to describe ...*

---

[1]neon ['niːɒn] [2]forehead ['fɔːhed, 'fɒrɪd] *Stirn* [3]melting pot ['meltɪŋ pɒt] *Schmelztiegel* [4]spoonful ['spuːnfʊl] *ein Löffel* [5]Lancashire ['læŋkəʃə] *Grafschaft im Nordwesten Englands* [6]dollop ['dɒləp] *Klacks* [7]pinch [pɪnʃ] *Prise* [8]season ['siːzn] *würzen* [9]sprinkle *hier: leichter Einschlag/leichte Färbung* [10]Scandinavian [ˌskændɪ'neɪviən] [11]spirit *Geist* [12]cheeky *frech, schnippisch* [13]genetics [dʒə'netɪks] *Genetik* [14]eyebrow ['aɪbraʊ] *Augenbraue* [15]brush stroke ['brʌʃ strəʊk] *Pinselstrich* [16]crooked ['krʊkɪd] *schief* [17]predict [prɪ'dɪkt] *voraussagen* [18]molasses [məʊ'læsɪz] *Melasse, dunkelbrauner Zuckersirup* [19]rust *Rost* [20]beast [biːst] *Tier* [21]tame *zähmen*

## 5 Creating imagery ➔ *SB (p. 15)*

Look at the two photos. In your exercise book, describe the girl and the boy (e.g. how they look, what they might be like, how they live and talk, how they might feel, what their hobbies are ...). Use metaphors and similes. Write about 100 words.

*The girl in the first photo wants people to think she's as ...*

## 6 ACCESS TO WORDS Describing a person's identity ➔ *SB (p. 16) • Wordbank 1*

a) Choose five words from the box that you might want to use in your talk in c). In your exercise book, write sentences that explain what they mean.

African-American · aggressive · ambitious · athletic · competitive · conservative · conventional · determined · emotional · famous · gay · gentle · honest · kind · liberal · musical · optimistic · original · passionate · patient · patriotic · reliable · responsible · self-confident · straight · tolerant · tough

*1 A reliable person is always there when you need him/her.*

*2 Someone who is musical is very good at singing or playing an instrument.*

b) In your exercise book, rewrite the sentences below to make the meaning stronger or weaker. Use adverbs and adjectives from the box.

(not) particularly · huge · terribly · (not) very · great · big · quite

**TIP:** Remember: you can search for collocations using quotation marks in a search engine. If you don't get many results, the collocation may not be very common.

1 He's the sort of person who is patient with others.

*He's the sort of person who is particularly patient with others.*

2 She's proud of her liberal upbringing.

3 One thing he values is adventure.

4 He's a fan of the African-American author Maya Angelou.

5 She likes volunteering.

6 She loves to read novels, but she isn't a fan of poetry.

7 They don't find indoor climbing interesting.

8 Music has always been important to him.

c) ● Prepare a two-minute talk for your class about someone you know (or a famous person or character from a book). Describe how this person sees himself/herself. Before you start, make a list of 8–10 words from a) and b) that you want to use.

## 7 STUDY SKILLS Improving your electronic texts ➔ SB (p. 17) • SMC 15 (p. 67)

**a) ○ Tick (✓) the statements that are correct.**

1. Don't use more than one heading: they make a text look untidy. ☐
2. Any photos or pictures used should fit the amount of text and the font size. ☐
3. Empty lines between paragraphs are a waste of space. ☐
4. It's all right to use different fonts for the captions and the body of the text. ☐
5. Margins should be used above and below the text as well as at the sides. ☐
6. All images must include the photographer's name. ☐
7. Standard fonts such as Arial are best. ☐
8. Use different styles (e. g. bold and italics) to make the text visually more inviting. ☐

**b) Re-read the guidelines on p. 17 of your student's book on text layout and formatting. Note down in your exercise book the five most important things you want to remember next time you write an electronic text.**

– not too much text on page ...

**c) ● Examine the text below. Mark the parts of the text that do not follow the guidelines. You can also write keywords or short notes. Tell your partner what you would change, and why.**

**Hollie McNish**

Hollie McNish is a British poet, writer and spoken-word performer. She was born in Reading, in southern England.        Hollie first began writing poetry when she was seven but did not perform her poems on stage until she was in her twenties. Soon after that, she won several poetry competitions and became UK Slam Poetry Champion in 2009. *Hollie MCnish's poems are inspiring, powerful and written from the heart using everyday language and humour to capture her feelings. Her work is easy to understand, and she comes across as very honest. This is perhaps why up to one thousand people attend each of her live performances.* She is also very popular online, with certain videos of her reciting her poemsgoing viral and receiving  milions of views. Her published books include *Papers*, **Nobody Told Me**, Cherry Pie and *Plum*. SHe has also recorded an album of poetry called Versus. Hollie McNish also co-wrote the play *Offside*, whichis about the history of women's football in the UK.

        Hollie McNish has worked with other poets and spoken-word artists including Kae Tempest. She has also been involved in many poetry workshops and projects at schools. One interestingproject was at a high school, where she helped pupils to decorate their new school building with lines from poems they had written. (Photo: from the internet)

## 8 WORDS How to structure an opinion piece ➔ SB (p. 19)

**○ Complete the text using words from the box. There are three more words than you need.**

action · captions · catch · facts · fonts · ~~headline~~ · job · long · main · opinion · paragraph · provocative · quotes · statement · supporting · topic

Your headline can have different forms – a question, a __________ or a solution – but it must __________ the reader's attention. The __________ of the first __________ is to make him or her want to keep reading. Make sure it is not too __________. Both your __________ and opinion should be stated clearly. You can then use __________ paragraphs to add information that backs up your __________ statement. Do this by using __________, statistics or other __________ in the paragraphs. Finally, use the conclusion to remind the reader of your __________ and suggest a solution or call for __________.

## 9 REVISION Ending discrimination in sport (Simple present, simple past, modals) ➔ SB (p. 20)

a) ● Re-read section 5 on p. 20 of your student's book. Then read the paragraph, looking carefully at the verbs. What mistakes can you find? Underline them in the text.

Women and men now has equal status in almost all areas of professional life, so why is the pay gap still existing in sport? It simply does not makes sense. In 2022, there were only two women on the list of the fifty highest paid athletes: tennis players Naomi Osaka (19th) and Serena Williams (31st). In soccer, except for in a couple of countries such as the US, Australia and Norway, very few national teams pay men and women the same. You know that in 2021 the men's winning team in the UK FA Cup have got £1.8 m but the women's winning team have received just 1.4 % of that – £25,000? These is just a couple of examples of a huge gender pay gap in international sport. I am surprised that information like this do not make people angrier. Doesn't every woman has the right to receive fair pay? I am believing that the equal rights movement in sport still have a long way to go.

b) Check your answers with a partner. Then write a corrected version of the text in your exercise book.

c) Decide which of these statements express support for ending discrimination in sport. Then, in your exercise book, rewrite the other sentences so that they also express the same thing.

1 We should accept racism on the football pitch. ☐
2 International sports competitions ought to pay men and women the same. ☐
3 We absolutely must keep protesting against discrimination in sport. ☐
4 Female athletes can be expected to work for less than male athletes. ☐
5 We have to accept the idea that things will never change. ☐
6 Governments around the world should not ignore anti-racism groups. ☐
7 We ought to listen to people who support unequal pay. ☐
8 No successful athlete should earn less just because she is a woman. ☐

## 10 Using persuasive language ➔ SB (p. 21)

○ Underline the correct answer.

1 **Persuasion techniques:**
are words that make your reader feel angry or sad / are a useful device for improving your style and winning over your reader / suggest that your arguments are based on facts.

2 **Using rhetorical questions:**
stresses your point / makes the reader consider another point of view / shows that other people agree with you.

3 **Dramatic statistics are used to:**
get closer to your reader / underline important points / refer to events from history.

4 **Using the personal pronoun *we*:**
shows how strongly you feel / shows that everyone has the same opinion / suggests that you have something in common with your readers.

5 **Anecdotes:**
suggest that your argument is factual / show that you know the topic well / let you get closer to your reader.

## 11 Analysing an opinion piece ➜ SB (pp. 19–21) • SF8 (p. 62)

**Look at the guidelines on pp. 19–21 of your student's book. Do you think the text below includes all the points? Write notes in your exercise book to justify your answer.**

*1 headline must capture reader's attention*

### Gendered[1] toys are dangerous!

For years, toy companies have advertised[2] cars, trucks and superhero costumes to boys, while we have been encouraged to buy dolls[3], toy kitchens and princess dresses for girls. But it is ridiculous to suggest that all children of one sex[4] like a certain kind of toy – and it is dangerous.

Gendered toys are so normal in our society that many of us do not even notice what is happening. My five-year-old cousin plays with dolls at home, but he would never tell his friends, because they think dolls are just for girls. And I know a little girl who loves cars but avoids[5] playing with them at nursery[6] because people say they are "boys' toys". Children should not have to feel ashamed[7] like this in the 21st century. Most women drive, and a father pushing his baby along in a buggy[8] is now a common sight[9]. So, we really ought not to let toy companies tell our children what they should like based on old-fashioned ideas.

When children feel that they cannot live their lives the way they want, it affects[10] their identity, and this can have a serious impact[11] on their self-confidence. The UK children's organization *ChildLine* reports that low self-esteem[12] is a growing problem: between 2014 and 2020 the number of counselling[13] sessions provided[14] by *ChildLine* for children with low self-esteem and mental health issues rose from 35,000 to 55,000. As if this were not worrying enough, gendered toys can also affect children's education, since different kinds of toys teach different skills. Therefore, experts say that children should play with the widest possible range[15] of toys. Who could argue with that?

Companies say it is traditional to separate children by sex. But did you know that until the 1970s, most toys came in bright colours such as red or yellow? A red ball could be for both boys and girls, so siblings[16] could share it. But now, toy companies can sell more if parents think their son needs a blue ball and their daughter must have a pink one.

The good news is that some parents and politicians[17] have decided to do something. There are now movements around the world that want to break down the pink/blue divide[18]. In the UK, a group called *Let Toys Be Toys* works to make toy shops stop describing products[19] as "girls' toys" and "boys' toys". In the USA, there are also groups that take the issue very seriously.

These are all positive actions, but the situation is so dangerous that I think we ought to stop buying all toys that are advertised as being just for boys or just for girls. Today the UK is the largest toy market in Europe, so if we stopped buying gendered toys, perhaps toy companies would finally start to listen.

---

[1]gendered toy [ˌdʒendəd 'tɔɪ] *Spielzeug, das durch seine Aufmachung gezielt Jungen oder Mädchen ansprechen soll* [2]advertise sth. ['ædvətaɪz] *für etw. Werbung machen* [3]doll [dɒl] *Puppe* [4]sex [seks] *Geschlecht* [5]avoid [ə'vɔɪd] *vermeiden* [6]nursery ['nɜːsri] *Kindergarten* [7]feel ashamed [ə'ʃeɪmd] *sich schämen* [8]buggy ['bʌgi] *Kinderwagen* [9]sight [saɪt] *Anblick* [10]affect [ə'fekt] *sich auswirken* [11]impact ['ɪmpækt] *Einfluss* [12]low self-esteem [ləʊ ˌselfɪ'stiːm] *geringes Selbstwertgefühl* [13]counselling ['kaʊnslɪŋ] *Beratungs-* [14]provide [prə'vaɪd] *zur Verfügung stellen* [15]range [reɪndʒ] *Spektrum* [16]sibling ['sɪblɪŋ] *Geschwister (meist pl.)* [17]politician [ˌpɒlə'tɪʃn] *Politiker/in* [18]divide [dɪ'vaɪd] *Kluft* [19]product ['prɒdʌkt] *Produkt*

## 12 Work and identity ➜ SB (pp. 19–21) • SF 8 (p. 62)

a) Complete the following sentence in as many ways as you can: Jobs and work can be important for people's identities because …

– … *people usually spend most of their lives working.*

– …

b) ● In your exercise book, write an opinion piece on whether jobs and work are important for people's identities. Write about 300 words. Consider the guidelines on pp. 19–21 of your student's book.

c) ● Give your text to a partner to read. Get feedback on the structure, grammar and style, e.g. headline, conclusion, use of tenses, persuasion techniques.

d) ● Think of improvements you could make. Then edit your text and read it.

## 13 On the news (The passive: present progressive form) ➜ SB (p. 24)

A radio journalist is reporting from a science and technology fair. Complete her sentences using the present progressive passive.

1 All the different projects *are being set up* (set up).

2 Visitors ______ (give) a plan of the fair as they arrive.

3 An amazing new kind of engine ______ (present) at this stand.

4 We ______ (take) to meet last year's winner.

5 I have a tiny camera here and I ______ (show) how to use it.

6 Lots of new devices ______ (test) at the fair today.

7 How exciting – the winners ______ (announced) right now on the stage!

8 I ______ (lead) backstage now to interview the winners.

## 14 Protecting your information online ➜ SB (p. 24) • SMC 16–18 (p. 68)

a) ● 02 You will hear a German radio report about teens and online security. Before listening, explain these German words in English in your exercise book:

Identitätsmissbrauch | Sachschaden | Strafanzeige | Privatsphäre

Then listen. Take notes on the dangers of posting party invitations online.

b) ● You are chatting online with Connor, your school's Canadian exchange student. He is planning a party when his German host family is away. He tells you he wants to post about it on social media. Tell him in English about the report you heard and what could happen if he posted the family's address online. Write about 100 words in your exercise book.

*Connor, I really don't think you should …*

## 15 We can read DNA as if it was a text (Clauses of manner; clauses of purpose) ➜ SB (p. 25)

Connect the sentence halves using the words in the box.
Write the complete sentences in your exercise book.

as if · as though · like · so · so that

1 'Designer babies' makes the topic of gene editing sound
2 Scientists can use Crispr
3 Countries need to cooperate
4 All this talk of DNA makes it seem
5 We're meeting at the library this evening
6 Gene research should be shared between countries

A unethical genetic research is forbidden everywhere.
B we can study for our Biology exam.
C it weren't a serious issue.
D all of humanity can benefit.
E it was a chemical scissors to cut DNA at precise locations.
F humans are recipes or computer programs.

## 16 The meaning behind the flags ➜ SB (p. 26) • SMC 32 (pp. 74)

a) ● In your exercise book, describe the photos. Write about 30 words about each one.

*Photo 1 shows an athlete ...*

b) ● What are the reasons for using the flags in each photo?
In your exercise book, write three to four sentences for each picture.

1

3

2

4

5

*In photo 1 it looks as if ...*
*The flags are there because they express/stand for ...*

## 17 Flags and identity ➜ SB (p. 26) • SMC 26 (p. 71)

**a)** You are going to listen to a podcast about flags in New Zealand. In Access 5, you learnt about the country. Refresh your memory by matching the words with their description. There is one description you do not need.

**TIP:** In a listening task, it is helpful to brainstorm any knowledge you have on the given topic, e.g. New Zealand, before listening.

**a** Māori
**b** Aotearoa
**c** Pākehā
**d** Waitangi

**1** The indigenous name for the kiwi bird, native to New Zealand.
**2** The name used by the indigenous people to describe New Zealanders descended from (mainly European) settlers.
**3** The indigenous people of New Zealand.
**4** The place where a treaty was signed between the indigenous tribes of New Zealand and the British Empire.
**5** New Zealand in the language of the indigenous people.

**b)** 03 First read the task. While you are listening to the podcast, circle the correct answer. Then listen again and check your answers.

1 Flags can be difficult topics, especially in …
- **A** new states or countries.
- **B** countries with a troubled past.
- **C** countries at war.

2 The design of the Māori flag, *Te Kara*, included …
- **A** the Union Jack.
- **B** the flag of England.
- **C** thirteen white stars.

3 After the Treaty of Waitangi, the *Te Kara* was …
- **A** replaced by the Union Jack as the national flag.
- **B** adopted as the national flag of New Zealand.
- **C** made illegal and couldn't be shown.

4 The New Zealand Ensign became the national flag in …
- **A** 1892.
- **B** 1902.
- **C** 1922.

5 Since 2009, the Māori *Tino* flag can be flown …
- **A** above the New Zealand Ensign.
- **B** instead of the New Zealand Ensign.
- **C** beside the New Zealand Ensign.

6 The Union Jack in the Ensign flag …
- **A** confuses people.
- **B** is part of the country's proud heritage.
- **C** makes it seem as if the country is still a British possession.

7 The silver fern flag was supported by …
- **A** 43 % of New Zealand voters.
- **B** 34 % of New Zealand voters.
- **C** 57 % of New Zealand voters.

8 The latest studies show New Zealanders …
- **A** are more in favour of becoming a republic.
- **B** want a referendum on becoming a republic.
- **C** are less in favour of the monarchy than they were.

**c)** Now write the correct names under the four flags. If you need to, listen to the podcast again.

New Zealand Ensign · Silver Fern · Te Kara · Tino

______________

______________

______________

______________

## 18 LISTENING COURSE Connected speech ➜ SB (p. 29) • SMC26 (p. 71)

a) 04 Read the sentences. Listen to how they are spoken in normal speech, then draw lines to link the words that are connected. Listen again and check.

1 Where is he? He should have been here by now!

2 I don't think there are any cakes left – sorry!

3 Tell her she'll have to wait. There's a big queue.

4 He's as old as her brother, but he looks younger.

5 Try and have a nice time – if you can.

6 I hope her dog's OK. He doesn't look well, does he?

b) 05 Read the sentences. Then listen to the sentences spoken at normal speed and write down the missing words. Listen again and check.

1 *Will he be* ______ going to your aunt's party?

2 How many times ______ London?

3 I sent ______ weeks ago.

4 ______ coming too?

5 ______ late again?

6 ______ this bottle, would you?

## 19 WORDS Poetry slams ➜ SB (p. 29)

Complete the sentences with words from the box in the correct form.

appeal to · consider · emphatic · expressive · focus on · gender · identity · importance · metaphor · original · passionate · perspective · poet · receive · simile · unlike

A poetry slam is a competition in which (1) *poets* read their (2) ______ work in front of an audience. The first poetry slams were held in Chicago in the 1980s. Slam poetry uses many of the traditional devices found in poetry, such as (3) ______ and (4) ______. But, (5) ______ traditional poetry, slam poetry (6) ______ using a person's (7) ______ to protest about social problems of great (8) ______, such as discrimination based on race or (9) ______. It is interesting to learn about these issues from different (10) ______, and that is one of the reasons why poetry slams (11) ______ so many people. The performers are very (12) ______ about their message. They use an (13) ______ style to catch the audience's attention and (14) ______ language to connect with them. The performers (15) ______ points from the audience. Slam poetry is still quite new, but it is already (16) ______ an art form.

## 1 WORDS A profile

**Complete the text with correct words, especially adverbs and adjectives as modifiers.**

My grandma Lin is the sort of person who r*eally* (1) likes to be around people. Her family is a **h**__________ (2) part of her life: she **a**__________ (3) loves visiting her children. She has always been a **f**__________ (4) hard-working person. She didn't have a **p**__________ (5) **c**__________ (6) career as a young woman: she was one of the first computer programmers at a large bank. She is **q**__________ (7) proud of what she achieved there. One person who **i**__________ (8) her was her father. He had his own company and was **e**__________ (9) hard-working. Maybe that's why she has always been so **a**__________ (10) and focused on success. One thing Grandma Lin values a **l**__________ (11) is music. She has always been **v**__________ (12) **p**__________ (13) about it and she is a **g**__________ (14) fan of the opera. I don't think she is very **m**__________ (15) herself, though: she says she's **n**__________ (16) **e**__________ (17) good at singing.

## 2 Why is he being photographed? (The passive: present progressive form)

**You are watching a film with your American host family, but you don't understand everything. Write questions in the present progressive passive in your exercise book.**

1 man/photograph/why/that

*Why is that man being photographed?*

2 arrest/scientists/why

3 car/her/stop/why

4 take/where/device

5 watch/that/why/woman

6 information/send/how

## 3 Writing an opinion piece: language structures (Simple present, simple past, modals)

**a) Read the statements about how to use different tenses in an opinion piece. Tick (✓) the statements that are correct.**

1 For general statements, the simple present is often used. ☐

2 When you give examples from your experience, you should only use the simple past. ☐

3 You can use the simple present to support your argument with examples from research. ☐

**b) Kyle believes that technology that identifies us is very scary. He thinks that people should do something about the issue, so he has written an opinion piece. Underline the correct modal verb.**

1 We **mustn't / might / could** let companies have access to our personal information.

2 People **can't / ought to / may** learn to protect their smartphones.

3 We **needn't / should / can't** realize that we pay for 'free' services with our private information.

4 The problem is that some programs **should / can / ought to** identify us in the street – that is creepy.

5 Nobody **have to / needn't / has to** accept this, though – we have a choice.

6 I think people **need / shouldn't / must** wake up and realize that it's time to change things.

## 4 Writing an opinion piece: tips for Maddison

Your Australian friend Maddison wants to write an opinion piece for her school magazine.
She has never written one before. Write her an email with a list of tips.
Give advice on structure and style. Write about eight tips.

*Hi Maddison! Here are the tips I wanted to send you.*

- *Use a headline that catches the reader's attention.*
- *You should ...*
- *...*

*Let me read it when you've finished!*

## 5 Money and identity: writing an opinion piece

a) Consider why money can be important for people's identities.
In your exercise book, express your view in a few sentences, e.g.:

*Rich people have a responsibility to help the world's poor.
And being generous makes us happier too.*

*Advertisements try to make us buy things to become a certain kind of person.
But we are more than what we own.*

b) Write an opinion piece about money and identity on your computer.
Write about 300 words. Consider your tips from exercise 4.

## Check: Writing

a) Vergleiche deine Antworten mit den Lösungen auf Seite 87 im Workbook.
b) Schätze deine Antworten mit einem grünen oder roten Gesicht ein.

| | ☺ | ☹ | |
|---|---|---|---|
| 1 Hast du in Aufgabe 1 Vokabeln gewusst, die dir helfen, über Identität zu sprechen und ein Profil zu schreiben? | ○ | ○ | → 1 |
| 2 Hast du in Aufgabe 2 das Passiv des *present progressive* richtig eingesetzt? | ○ | ○ | → 2 |
| 3 Hast du in Aufgabe 3 gewusst, wie man in einem *opinion piece* die Zeitformen und Modalverben richtig verwendet? | ○ | ○ | → 3 |
| 4 Hast du in Aufgabe 4 und Aufgabe 5 gewusst, wie man ein *opinion piece* mit korrekter Struktur und im richtigen Stil schreibt? | ○ | ○ | → 4 |

c) Wenn du dich rot eingeschätzt hast, schau dir die rechte Spalte an.
Die Nummern führen dich zu den passenden Übungen im Skills Training (S. 14–15).
Dort kannst du gezielt Writing trainieren.

## 1 WORDS Writing a profile

**a) Find the missing adjectives from this unit.**

1 A person who is ______________________ about poetry really loves poems.

2 Someone who is good at all sports is very ______________________.

3 Some dogs are gentle, and others are quite ______________________.

4 If you like to do things the same way as everyone else, you're ______________________.

5 She comes from a very ______________________ family: they all play instruments.

6 We don't know much about him: he's quite ______________________.

7 Her parents are often open to new ideas: they're quite ______________________.

8 I've read books like that before. The story isn't very ______________________.

**b) Underline the correct modifier in each sentence.**

1 Tom is a **really / huge / fairly** fan of American football.

2 My upbringing was not **fairly / particularly / not a lot** conventional.

3 Technology isn't a **really / bit / big** part of her life.

4 One thing I value **a lot / really / quite** is time with my family.

5 My friends think I'm **great / quite / a lot** reliable.

6 Their dialect isn't **absolutely / very / not particularly** easy to understand.

**c) In your exercise book, write a profile of a friend or member of your family. Use adverbs and adjectives as modifiers. Write about 150 words.**

## 2 A football match (The passive: present progressive form)

**A journalist is reporting from a women's World Cup match. Complete his sentences using the present progressive passive.**

1 This match ______________________ (watch) by millions around the world.

2 Today you ______________________ (show) the very best of women's football!

3 The Swedish goalkeeper ______________________ (test) today.

4 The teams ______________________ (lead) onto the pitch for the second half.

5 The USA's best player ______________________ (give) a red card.

6 The winners ______________________ (interview) by the international media.

7 A trophy ______________________ (bring) onto the pitch.

8 The winners ______________________ (photograph) by thousands of fans.

## 3 Animal rights (Simple present, simple past, modals)

**a) Read the paragraph, looking carefully at the verb tenses.
In your exercise book, correct the mistakes you find.**

People are sometimes asking whether animals ought to has more rights. I believe they should. Sadly, it is a fact that cruel treatment of animals is something that happen in every country around the world, in zoos, homes and the fashion industry, among others. On average, every 30 seconds someone in England and Wales is calling the RSPCA – the UK's organization for protecting animals. In 2007, the Animal Welfare Act has became law in England, but the problem is still existing. In 2022 the RSPCA has received over one million phone calls about animals that have needed help. In the same year, it rescued almost 130,000 animals. Many people are thinking that the law still does not protect animals enough.

**b) Look carefully at the modals in the sentences below. In your exercise book, rewrite the sentences so that they express support for animal rights.**

1 Companies that test make-up on animals needn't pay a fine.

2 We might ignore the fact that many zoo animals live in terrible conditions.

3 People can stop protesting against the cruel treatment of animals.

4 Some industries do not consider animal rights important, but we may accept this.

## 4 Work and identity: editing your text ➜ *SMC 8 (p. 62)*

You are going to edit the opinion piece that you wrote for exercise 5b) on p. 13.

**a) Re-read your text. Does it include everything from the checklist below?
Tick (✓) every step that you have completed.**

| | |
|---|---|
| 1 Have you written an interesting headline that catches the reader's attention? | ○ |
| 2 Is the first paragraph short? | ○ |
| 3 Have you stated your opinion and topic clearly in the first paragraph? | ○ |
| 4 Have you backed up your main statement with | |
| – statistics | ○ |
| – historical facts | ○ |
| – quotes | ○ |
| – anecdotes? | ○ |
| 5 Have you included the personal pronouns *I*, *you* or *we*? | ○ |
| 6 Have you used expressive language? | ○ |
| 7 Does your text contain at least one rhetorical question? | ○ |
| 8 Are the verbs used correctly? | ○ |
| 9 Do the modals express what you want them to express? | ○ |
| 10 Does your conclusion restate your opinion and then offer a solution/call to action? | ○ |

**b) Edit your text so that all the steps in the checklist are complete, then read your text again.**

### Part one: Before listening

**Step 1: Your first look at the exam**
In a listening exam, first read the introduction and all the questions from beginning to end quickly. Use a pencil to highlight vocabulary or questions that do not seem clear to you.

**Step 2: Reducing the number of surprises**
Now, go back to the title and short introduction text. You can reduce the number of surprises by thinking about what you can expect to hear.

**TIP:** The time before listening is just as important as the time you spend listening.

**TIP:** All the information you need to answer the tasks will be in the audio text, so do not worry if the theme of the listening is one you do not know very well, e.g. sport in South Africa.

## 1 What to expect

**Read the titles and contexts 1–4 below. Under the introductions, make notes about what you could expect. Consider things like number of speakers, accents, themes, vocabulary, etc. The first is done for you.**

1 You are on a walking tour of Auckland. As you enjoy discovering New Zealand's largest city, listen to the audio guide.

*One speaker, non-British accent, historical themes/facts, descriptive city vocabulary, …*

2 It is difficult to find a city more obsessed with football than Manchester in the Northwest of England. Listen to a radio interview with Manchester United's biggest fan about the reasons for the city's love of the game.

_______________________________________________

3 *Born a Crime* is the story of Trevor Noah's childhood in South Africa during the Apartheid era. Find out more about Trevor from the beginning of the audiobook.

_______________________________________________

4 Should we be afraid of AI (artificial intelligence)? A radio programme heard the views of shoppers on the 'Golden Mile', the busiest shopping district in New Zealand's capital city, Wellington.

_______________________________________________

**Step 3: Identifying the type of task**
Read the tasks carefully to understand what you need to do.

## 2 Types of task

**Match the each of the four task types below to the correct description. Draw lines.**

| Task type | | What you need to do |
|---|---|---|
| **Closed format** | Multiple choice | Show that you understand the general meaning of what each speaker said by choosing the correct heading or description. |
| | Matching | Summarise information from the listening text to complete a sentence or answer a question. Use as few words as possible. You do not have to use the exact words of the listening text. |
| **Semi-open format** | Fill in | Understand first the difference between the three possible answers, then listen closely to find the right one. |
| | Short answer | Listen in a very concentrated way and identify the exact missing word(s). |

**TIP:** A task might include a mixture of task types, e.g. a monologue may have some multiple choice and some fill in questions. A dialogue may have multiple choice and matching tasks.

Part two: Task types in detail

## 3 Multiple choice

You are going to listen to short extracts from different listening tasks.
Each extract has one multiple choice question for you to answer.

**TIP:** Answer every question, even if you are not sure.

a) Before you listen, read the questions. For a–c, brainstorm words that could express the same or a similar meaning as the underlined key words. The first question is done for you. Write in your exercise book.

1 Today, visitors to Merrion Square find a …

- **A** residential area. *homes/flats/living*
- **B** fashionable area. *trendy/cool/'in' district*
- **C** business area. *offices/factories/industry*

2 AI is being used by the teachers to …

- **A** assist students with homework.
- **B** recognise students' needs.
- **C** provide information to parents.

3 Thomas Hutchinson was the first to present crisps …

- **A** with different tastes.
- **B** in small packets.
- **C** as a light meal.

4 Patricia White had to give up singing because …

- **A** she was expecting a baby.
- **B** she was in a car crash.
- **C** of troubles with her voice.

b) 06 Now listen to the recording and do questions 1–4 in a). You can listen twice.

## 4 Fill in and short answer

You are going to listen to an audio text and do a fill in and a short answer task. Before you listen, do a) and b). In part c), you will listen and complete the exercises. With fill in and short answer tasks, the words around the gap or in the sentence can help to guide you.

a) Highlight the key words in 1–6 below.

b) Think about what could fill the gap or what kind of information could finish the sentences in 1–6. Make notes in your exercise book.

*In number 1, the first gap is probably a person/people and the second gap could be ...*

*In number 4, the grandfather must say something surprising or shocking ...*

Fill in

1 The narrator and ______________ are at a meeting place in the ______________ Wellington city.

2 The narrator has been waiting ______________________________ to hear some news.

3 Koro Aata, the grandfather, says the last such meeting happened ______________________.

Short answer

4 Listening to his grandfather, the narrator is surprised because ______________________

______________________________________________

5 When the grandfather has finished on the phone, he reacts ______________________.

6 The narrator's grandmother, however, ______________________.

c) 07 Now listen to the text. It is a short narrative text from the beginning of a story set in New Zealand. Complete 1–6 above. You can listen twice.

## 5 Matching

In this task, you may hear several people talking about one particular issue or theme. You will be given short summaries or statements and asked to match them to the speakers. There may be one or two extra statements that do not belong to any speaker.

a) Look at the tables below. Read the context of the listening.

b) 08 Now look at the key words box. Listen to the recording and match the key words/phrases to the speakers. Write them in the 'key words' column.

c) Read the summaries and listen to the recording again. The key words should help you to write the number of the speaker into the box beside the matching summary. There is one more summary than you need.

**Context:** New Zealand is one of the 15 Commonwealth countries that recognize King Charles III as their head of state. Five New Zealanders were asked if the country should now cut its ties with the monarchy and become a republic.

**Key words**
as soon as possible · bad timing · both sides · eventually · Kiwi head of state · lose our identity · other issues · proud · royals are positive · wouldn't change

| Speakers | Key words |
|---|---|
| 1 Bob | |
| 2 Mary | *as soon as possible/* |
| 3 Carol | |
| 4 Rawiri | |
| 5 Emma | |

| Should New Zealand become a republic? Summaries of the speakers' views | Which speaker? |
|---|---|
| A Undecided and not very interested. | |
| B Yes, but in the future. | |
| C Not in favour and nobody really wants it. | |
| D Against the idea – it's part of Kiwi identity. | |
| E Believes New Zealand should have a Māori King | |
| F In favour and it should happen immediately. | |

### Part three: More practice

In this section, do the exercises as if you were in an exam.

## 6 The Liverpool pound

You are planning a trip to Liverpool. You find a podcast containing a report on the Liverpool pound.

a) 09 Listen and answer questions 1–7.

1 Local currencies are accepted as payment …

**A** in every store and firm in a specific region.

**B** and replace the normal forms of money.

**C** by stores and firms which take part in the scheme.

2 In the UK, local currencies …

**A** can take different forms in different places.

**B** all work in the same way.

**C** are only available in electronic form.

3 A city can benefit from a local currency because …

**A** people buy more things when they use it.

**B** people save money using it.

**C** it makes the city wealthier when people use it.

4 A local currency can also …

**A** create a better sense of community.

**B** give a boost to the economy and create jobs.

**C** make it easy for friends to send money to each other.

5 The organisers of local currencies market them as a way to show ______________________ your area.

6 Some currencies use ______________________ to encourage residents to feel good about their home.

7 Name one drawback of a local currency scheme. ______________________

______________________.

b) Do this task **after** you have listened to the whole report. (Circle) the correct answer.

Which motto fits best to currencies such as the Liverpool pound?

**A** Shop local, save the planet **B** Local money for local problems **C** Spend with pride, support your city

c) Listen to the extract again so you can check your answers.

## 7 The Theatre of Dreams

10 You are going to hear an interview with Tina Smith, the author of a book about one of the UK's biggest and most-loved football clubs. Listen and answer the questions.

1 According to one report, Manchester United has ______________________ supporters around the globe.

2 The name of Tina's book was inspired by a name given to ______________________ by its supporters.

3 Tina believes that football grew in importance for people as …

**A** the region's economy became worse. **B** the city became bigger and bigger. **C** the war made life harder.

4 The 'Class of '92' is the name given to the players who, in 1992, joined the professional team and ______________________

______________________.

5 The achievement that stands out for Tina was in 1999 when …

**A** the club made Alex Ferguson the manager. **B** it won three competitions. **C** it won every game it played.

6 The English women's national team are currently ______________________.

## 8 The British Empire

a) 11 You will hear five British people give their views on the British Empire. While listening, match the descriptions A to G with the speakers 1 to 5. There are two more headings than you need.

**A** Regrets that there is no British Empire today.

**1** Jane

**B** Ashamed of what the Empire did.

**2** Purnit

**C** Proud that the Empire helped all of humanity develop.

**3** Kingsley

**D** Annoyed that people look back at the past – we should look forwards.

**4** Siobhán

**E** Thinks that all empires were bad.

**5** Peter

**F** Angry that the Empire's negative effects can be seen in today's Britain.

**G** Proud of the Empire's achievements.

b) Listen to the recording again so you can check your answers.

# What makes a community?

## 1 Technology and community

→ SB (pp. 32–33) • SMC32 (pp. 74)

a) ○ Look at the photos.
- Describe the setting, the people and what they are doing.
- Why do you think they have come together?
- How might these activities make them feel part of a community?

Write in your exercise book.

1

2

3

4

*Picture 1 shows a group of people talking ... They seem to be in a ... I think they have come together to ... This activity might make them feel part of a community because ...*

b) Look at the following pairs of activities. Choose one pair and explain which activity you would prefer to do, and why. Consider aspects such as fun, costs, time, etc. Write about 100–150 words in your exercise book.

1 staying in touch with your friends via social media – meeting your friends to chat and play games

*Staying in touch with friends via social media is easy because ...*
*But I also think it's easier to concentrate on what someone is saying if you are ...*
*I would prefer to meet my friends to chat and play games because ...*

2 supporting a foreign football team and watching their matches on TV or online – supporting a local football team and going to their matches

3 doing yoga at home with online videos – going to a yoga class near your home

4 buying most things you need online – buying most things from the local shops

c) ● Comment on this statement. Justify your answer. Write about 150–200 words in your exercise book.

> "Technology is destroying our feeling of community."

## 2 STUDY SKILLS Analysing a text ➔ SB (p. 37) • SMC 1 (p. 60)

**a) Read this excerpt from the first chapter of the novel *Butterfly* by David Fermer. The novel tells the fictional story of Noemi Petersen, a teenage climate activist from South Africa. When you have read it, do tasks b)–f) on the next page.**

### ≈ The End ≈

A loud hammering wakes me from my sleep. Bang! Bang! Bang! Someone is hitting our front door as if the house were on fire.

What's going on?

I hear shouts in the dark. A man's voice.

"Mr Petersen? Mrs Petersen? Open the door!"

Dad comes out of his bedroom. I hear Mum asking, "Who is it?"

"I don't know," Dad says.

I look at my phone. It's 3 o'clock in the morning!

Dad opens the front door.

"State Security," says the man, his voice quiet now. "We have to speak to your daughter. Where is she?"

"In bed." Dad doesn't understand. "What's this about?"

I hear footsteps coming towards my room. The door opens, cutting the darkness with light. Two people step into my room, their faces dark. I hold Winnie close to my chest. As if my old teddy bear could help me.

"Noemi Petersen?" A woman's voice from the shadows. "We have to talk to you."

I squeeze Winnie tighter. "Why? What have I done?"

"Get dressed, Miss Petersen," commands the man. "You're under arrest." […]

"Sit down, Noemi. We have a lot of questions."

I sit down at the kitchen table. The two State Security agents stand. Mum sits down next to me and puts her arm around my shoulders. Dad puts the kettle on. He looks scared.

The agents introduce themselves. The woman is called Agent Abara. The man is Agent Kalu. I have no idea why they are here.

Why? What do they think I've done? "Interview with Noemi Petersen," says the woman. "Seventeen years old. From Athlone, Cape Town. Noemi, can you tell us where you were yesterday evening at 6 pm?"

Yesterday evening? What day is today?

"Athlone Stadium," I say, because it's the truth.

"What were you doing there?"

"Meeting with the Environment Minister."

"Mr Edward Sisulu? Why?"

"I don't know. He wanted to see me."

The man gives a short laugh. "That's not what Mr Sisulu says."

"I don't understand," I tell them. "Mr Sisulu asked me to come to the car park outside the stadium before the game began. He wanted to speak to me."

Agent Kalu shakes his head. "Mr Sisulu says that you sent him a message asking him the same."

The woman swipes on her phone and shows me a screenshot of a message with my name on it sent to Edward Sisulu yesterday afternoon.

I never wrote that.

"The message was sent from your account," she says. "It was you who asked Mr Sisulu to meet you before the Santos match, not the other way around. Or are you calling the minister a liar?"

I can prove that's not true. "I need my phone," I say. "You can check it. It's on my bedside table."

The man goes to my room.

I think about my meeting with Sisulu yesterday evening. It was really strange. When we met, Sisulu acted as if he had no time to talk to me, even though it was his idea to meet, not mine.

"Why are you asking me all these questions?" I ask.

Agent Abara swipes her phone again to show me another photo, this time of a box containing something that looks like a car battery with an orange canister and a lot of red wires next to it.

"We found a bomb," the agent says. "Under the Minister's car."

Now I understand. They think it was me.

The two security agents ask me question after question. I show them the message Mr Sisulu sent me, but they say that doesn't prove I'm telling the truth.

"Who made the bomb?" they ask. "How did you plant it there? Why do you want to kill Mr Sisulu?"

I try to stay calm and think.

If Sisulu didn't send me that text, then who did? Someone is trying to set me up. I can see Agent Abara believes me, even if the man doesn't. It could be anybody. I have years of hate mail behind me. Threats from climate change deniers. People telling me I should focus on school instead and let the grown-ups deal with politics. Maybe someone is trying to send me to prison. Is that what this is all about?

I sit there trying to answer their questions, but there is nothing I can say which helps them. Then Agent Kalu's phone rings. He answers and listens to the caller, nodding his head.

"Good," he says. "Send me a photo."

After he hangs up, he turns to me and says, "They found fingerprints on the bomb. They belong to an 18-year-old old Swedish boy. Viggo Olofsson. Do you know him?"

My heart misses a beat. Of course I know Viggo.

b) Identify the text type and the narrative technique used by the author.

c) Underline which type of novel you think *Butterfly* could be.

1 Romance 2 Thriller/Mystery 3 Horror 4 Fantasy

d) Sometimes authors 'show' how characters feel and think indirectly by describing their actions. Sometimes they 'tell' us directly. First, decide whether these lines from the text are show or tell. Then, for the examples you have marked *show*, write in what you think are the character's inner thoughts or feelings.

| Line(s) | | show | tell | Character's inner thoughts or feelings |
|---|---|---|---|---|
| 14 | *Dad doesn't understand.* | | | |
| 21 | *I squeeze Winnie tighter.* | | | |
| 26 | *Mum sits down next to me and puts her arm around my shoulder.* | | | |
| 27–28 | *Dad puts the kettle on. He looks scared.* | | | |
| 42 | *The man gives a short laugh.* | | | |
| 79–80 | *I can see Agent Abara believes me, even if the man doesn't.* | | | |
| 71 | *Now I understand.* | | | |
| 95 | *My heart misses a beat.* | | | |

e) Look back at the excerpt. Read it again. Now think about your answers to b) and c). Why do you think the author chose this narrative technique for his novel? Think about the effect the technique has on you as a reader.

f) Would you like to read the novel? Say why/why not.

**EXTRA** Write the events in the excerpt from the perspective of the female security agent, Agent Abara.

## 3 Brandon said he was thinking about volunteering (Indirect speech) ➜ *SB (p. 38)*

**Brandon from California is thinking about volunteering in Peru, South America, and he talks to his brother, Sam, about it. Imagine you are Sam. You visit your grandmother a few days after your talk with Sam. Tell her what Brandon said.**

1 "I considered going to Spain but decided to go to South America instead."

______________________________________________

______________________________________________

2 "A friend of mine went to Peru last year and she had the experience of a lifetime."

______________________________________________

______________________________________________

3 "It will be good for my Spanish and I can help people."

______________________________________________

______________________________________________

4 "I'm sure it won't be easy, but it will teach me new skills."

______________________________________________

______________________________________________

5 "Mum and Dad were surprised at first, but we talked about it yesterday and they agreed."

______________________________________________

______________________________________________

6 "I'm going to send my application tomorrow."

______________________________________________

______________________________________________

## 4 Getting to know the volunteers (Indirect speech: *advise, promise, suggest, …*) ➜ *SB (p. 38)*

**Brandon is in Peru and meets some of the other volunteers. Use a verb from the box to report what they said to him. Use each verb only once. Write in your exercise book.**

| |
|---|
| advise · *invite* · offer · promise · refuse · suggest · tell · ask |

1 Liz: "Come and eat with us, Brandon!"

*Liz invited Brandon to eat with them.*

2 Tim: "If you like, you can borrow my camera."

3 Liz: "Why don't we go swimming in the afternoon?"

4 Carlos: "I'll show you the community centre."

5 Carlos: "Rosa's grandfather lives there."

6 Tim: "If I were you, I'd just eat with your fingers."

7 Liz: "Do you miss your friends?"

8 Carlos: "I'm not eating your candy – yuck!"

## 5 Brandon has some questions (Indirect speech: *wh-* and *yes-no* questions) ➔ *SB (p. 39)*

Brandon asks some questions. Look at the answers. Write his questions in indirect speech.

1 *Brandon asked Carlos / wanted to know / wondered where ...*

Carlos said, "The village school is near the river."

2 ______

The teacher, Isabel, said, "You can help by putting these worksheets on the students' desks."

3 ______

Isabel told Brandon, "The children come from several different villages in the area."

4 ______

Isabel smiled and said, "Yes, I really enjoy my job."

5 ______

______

Isabel told him, "No, I've never been to the USA. But one day I will."

## 6 A phone call from South America (Indirect speech) ➔ *SB (p. 39)*

On a trip to a nearby city, Brandon phones his brother, Sam. Read these lines from their conversation. Imagine you are Sam again. Give your grandmother an update on Brandon's trip. Write in your exercise book.

1 Are the people in the village friendly? — The villagers are really friendly. — I feel part of the community already.

2 Where are you staying? — I'm staying with a family, in their house. — It's great!

3 How is your project going? — It's coming along really well. — Everyone thinks the community center will make a big difference.

4 Do you like the food? — I find it a little boring. — But it's healthy, at least.

5 When will you call again? — I don't know. — It'll probably be next month.

6 Will you visit any other countries before coming home? — No, I probably won't. — I'm going to travel to a few different cities, though.

1 *I asked Brandon / I wanted to know whether the people in the village were friendly. He said they were really friendly. He added that he felt part of the community already.*

## 7 LISTENING COURSE Different accents ➜ SB (p. 41) • SMC26 (p. 71)

a) ○ Think about the standard British and American English accents. Which accent has:

1 a weak **t**? ______________________ 3 a strong **t**? ______________________

2 a weak **r**? ______________________ 4 a strong **r**? ______________________

b) 12 Say the sentences as you think they would be in BE and AE, paying attention to the **r**s and **t**s. Record yourself. Then listen and check.

1 I'll buy a computer later.

2 I always drink cold water.

3 Does his daughter have a car?

4 The park there is much nicer.

## 8 LISTENING COURSE Standard BE and AE ➜ SB (p. 41) • SMC26 (p. 71)

a) ○ 13 You will hear six pairs of sentences. One speaker is British and the other is American. In each pair, one word is the same. Write it down.

1 ______________ 3 ______________ 5 ______________

2 ______________ 4 ______________ 6 ______________

b) 13 Listen again and repeat the sentences. Record yourself. Then listen and check.

c) 14 Say the words below as you think they would be pronounced in BE and AE. Listen and check.

lot – plant – enthusiastic – problem – plaster – obvious – mask – job – knew – basket

## 9 LISTENING COURSE Different British accents ➜ SB (p. 41) • SMC26 (p. 71)

a) ● 15 How might these words be pronounced in the following regional accents? Say each word in standard British pronunciation, then in the regional accent. Record yourself. Then listen and check.

1 bright (Scotland) 3 bath (England: north) 5 mouse (Northern Ireland)

2 scarf (England: west) 4 coat (Scotland) 6 shout (London/southeast)

b) 16 You will hear three university students talking about a community gardening project in London. Listen to their accents. Where are they from? Circle A, B or C.

**A** northern England, London, Scotland

**B** London, Northern Ireland, northern England

**C** Scotland, Northern Ireland, northern England

c) 16 Listen again. What are three advantages of having trees in the city?

______________________________________________

______________________________________________

______________________________________________

______________________________________________

## 10 While watching the plane land, ... (Participle clauses with *after, before, since,* ...) ➔ SB (p. 44)

○ Make one sentence out of two. Use participle clauses with the conjunction given. Write in your exercise book.

1 Alicia watches the missionaries' plane land. She talks to Joanna. (while)

*While watching the plane land, Alicia talks to Joanna.*

2 The missionaries get out of their plane. Then they take boxes of stuff into Angel's house. (after)

3 Joanna watches the missionaries eat. She gets angry. (while)

4 Brandon arrived in Peru in July. He has learned a lot about the country. (since)

5 Brandon phoned his brother. Then he played with the village kids. (after)

6 Brandon returned to the US. He organized a party in the village. (before)

## 11 Wanting to visit the missionaries, ... (Participle clauses meaning *because* ...) ➔ SB (p. 44)

a) ○ Match the main clauses on the left to a reason on the right.

| | |
|---|---|
| 1 Alicia goes to Angel's house because | she is very hungry. |
| 2 Joanna is almost drooling because | she knows the missionaries won't share. |
| 3 Margarita gives away her chocolate because | she sees her staring at it. |
| 4 Alicia just nods at Joanna because | they wanted to be comfortable. |
| 5 The missionaries have brought lots of stuff because | she wants to visit the missionaries. |
| 6 A missionary gave Joanna some chocolate because | she understands how Joanna feels. |

b) Rewrite the sentences you formed in a), using a participle clause (-ing ... / Not -ing ...) at the beginning of the sentence. Write in your exercise book.

1 *Wanting to visit the missionaries, Alicia goes to Angel's house.*

## 12 California Volunteers (Participle clauses meaning *and* ...) ➔ SB (p. 44)

○ Using participle clauses, rewrite each sentence in two different ways.
Write in your exercise book.

1 Our volunteers travel to different countries and offer support to local communities.

*Our volunteers travel to different countries, offering support to local communities.*
*Travelling to different countries, our volunteers offer support to local communities.*

2 The organization's volunteers live in villages and spend a lot of time with the locals.

3 Many of the young people try out new activities and develop new skills.

4 Brandon worked in Peru for six months and helped to build a community centre.

5 Stacey visits schools in California and advises students who are interested in volunteering.

6 Barbara works in a big office and supports the organization's director.

## 13 A book review: *The Help* 
→ SB (p. 42) • SMC 26 (p. 71)

a) You are going to listen to a podcast about books. It is divided into three parts. Read the tasks carefully before you listen. For each part, listen twice.

b) 17 Part one. Tick (✓) the correct box.

1 *The Help* belongs to the genre of …
- ☐ young adult fiction
- ☐ historical fiction
- ☐ crime fiction

2 The novel was published in …
- ☐ 2001
- ☐ 2006
- ☐ 2009

3 The title of the novel refers to …
- ☐ servants of wealthy families
- ☐ the lives of rich American families
- ☐ rich people helping poor people.

Civil Rights march, Jackson, Mississippi, 1966

c) 18 Part two. Complete the sentences.

1 In the novel, the story is ______________________ by three main characters.

2 An unusual aspect of *The Help* is that there's a ______________________ within the book.

3 A strength of the book is the different ______________________ it provides on the society at that time.

d) 19 Part three. Answer the questions. Write short answers.

1 What does the reviewer note about the author and the character Skeeter?

______________________________________________

______________________________________________

2 Why does the reviewer think *The Help* could be a good book to read on holiday?

______________________________________________

______________________________________________

3 For which group of readers does the reviewer strongly recommend the book?

______________________________________________

______________________________________________

**EXTRA** Listen to the whole podcast. Would you like to read the book? Say why (not). Write about 100 words in your exercise book.

**TIP:** When explaining whether you would like to read a novel, you can mention aspects such as:
- the plot
- the themes
- the setting
- the characters
- how the book makes the reader feel
- what the reader can learn from the book

## 14 *Collective action*: The repair café project ➔ *SB (p. 47) • SMC 16–17 (p. 68)*

You are part of a 'repair café' project and want to post information about it on an international youth-in-action website. Read the text below and write a short description in English for the website. Write complete sentences. Write about 80–100 words in your exercise book.

Unser im Januar 2021 gegründetes Repair-Café – eines von 300 in Deutschland – erfreut sich großer Beliebtheit. Zu jeder Veranstaltung empfangen wir ca. 40 Besucher. Wir und die rund 1500 Repair-Cafés weltweit verfolgen ein Ziel, nämlich unnötigen Müll zu vermeiden und somit der Wegwerfkultur den Kampf anzusagen. Auf diesem Wege bringen wir Menschen zusammen, die sich für die Umwelt engagieren wollen. Darüber hinaus besteht die Möglichkeit, handwerkliche Fähigkeiten zu erlernen, denn zahlreiche Freiwillige bieten anderen ihre Hilfe an, nicht mehr funktionsfähige Alltags- und Gebrauchsgegenstände zu reparieren. So haben wir bereits einige Wasserkocher, Fahrräder, Staubsauger, Lampen oder auch Kleidung und Spielzeug in Ordnung gebracht. Gelegentlich setzen wir sogar 3D-Drucker ein, um zerbrochene und nicht mehr verfügbare Bauteile herzustellen.

Starthilfe erhielten wir von einer in den Niederlanden ansässigen Organisation, die ein Netzwerk für alle, die ein eigenes Repair-Café gründen wollen, koordiniert. Die Idee des Repair-Café stammt auch aus den Niederlanden, wo 2009 das erste Repair-Café gegründet wurde.

*Our repair café was started in January 2021 ...*

## 15 We do need to make changes (Emphatic do) ➔ *SB (p. 48)*

There should only be one emphatic *do/did* in each sentence.
Decide which verb the speaker wants to emphasize and underline it.

1 It **makes / does make** a difference where the food we **buy / do buy** comes from.

2 Every kilometre a truck **drives / does drive** to deliver food **contributes / does contribute** to air pollution.

3 I think I **checked / did check** the label on the fruit when I **bought / did buy** it.

4 Peter **forgot / did forget** to buy milk, but he **remembered / did remember** to take the bottles for recycling.

5 Although the council **refused / did refuse** to cancel the new building, they **agreed / did agree** to make it more energy efficient.

## 16 Never has it been so urgent! ('Negative' adverbials + inversion) ➔ *SB (p. 48)*

Use the negative adverbials in brackets ( ) and inversion to make the sentences below logical.

1 The teenager had finished her speech, when the crowd burst into applause. (hardly)

*Hardly had the teenager finished her speech, when the crowd burst into applause.*

2 Auckland has seen such a large gathering of young, motivated climate protesters. (never)

______________________________

3 We handed in our petition, we also met with the prime minister. (not only)

______________________________

4 The country should open new coal mines. (under no circumstances)

______________________________

## 17 Ideas for saving water (The gerund after prepositions) ➔ SB (p. 49)

Complete these sentences from a website about saving water.
Use the correct preposition and the gerund of a verb in the box.

follow · save (2 x) · take · turn · use

1 We have plenty of ideas *for saving* water at home.

2 Many people are now deciding __________ baths: showers are better.

3 Have you ever thought __________ water from the shower again, to wash your car?

4 __________ off the tap when cleaning your teeth, you can save six litres per minute.

5 There are many advantages __________ water.

6 One good reason __________ these steps: you'll pay less for your water.

## 18 EXTRA Politics in the UK and the US ➔ SB (pp. 50–51) • SMC 1–2 (p. 60)

a) Underline the correct answers. You will find all the information you need on pp. 50–51 of your student's book.

Out of the three main branches of the UK government, only the **King / House of Commons / House of Lords** is elected by voters. The rules for voting depend on where you live. For example, you have to be 18 to vote in most parts of the UK, but **Scottish / Welsh / Northern Irish** people can vote at 16. Three out of four countries in the UK can vote for regional parliaments: the only one that cannot is **Northern Ireland / England / Wales**. Referendums are held **if enough voters want them / in Scotland only / on important topics only**.

In the USA, around **a quarter / a third / a fifth** of people are registered as a member of one of the big parties. This is often a requirement for **voting in a referendum / voting in the primaries / joining a pressure group**. Party members can try to get elected, but they must be **25 / 30 / 39** before they can be elected to the Senate. Referendums and initiatives to decide single issues are common at the **state / federal / presidential** level.

b) Naomi is 17 and Scottish. Lachlan is 18 and comes from the USA. Read the statements about their rights to vote and to get involved in politics. Tick (✓) the statements that are true. Write corrected versions of the false statements in your exercise book.

1 Being under 18, Naomi can't vote in any elections yet. ☐
2 Naomi is already old enough to join a party. ☐
3 Once Naomi is 18, she will have the right to stand for election to the House of Lords. ☐
4 Naomi can't vote for a head of state, but Lachlan can help to choose the next president. ☐
5 Naomi can't vote in an initiative because they don't exist in Scotland. ☐
6 Since Lachlan is already 18, he can vote in local, state and federal elections. ☐
7 If Lachlan joins a party, he can try to get elected to the House of Representatives. ☐
8 Lachlan will have to wait until he is 25 before he can organize an initiative at the federal level. ☐

c) ● Imagine you became a member of the *Bundestag*. What one thing would you do to make life better for young people? How/why would you do it? What would the advantages be for your local community? Write a short text outlining your ideas.

*If I were a member of the Bundestag, the one thing I would do to help young people*
*would be to make/create/give ...*

______________________________

______________________________

______________________________

______________________________

______________________________

______________________________

______________________________

______________________________

______________________________

## 19 WORDS A profile of a young MP ➜ *SB (pp. 50–51) • Wordbank 4*

Fill in the gaps with the correct words from the box. Each word is used only once.

> avoid · campaign · capital · causes · commons · donate · dynamic · elect · election · emphasize · involvement · MP · parliament · party · policies · political · politician · referendum · stand

Nadia Whittome was ______________ to the UK's House of ______________ in 2019 aged 23, making her the youngest ______________, or 'Baby of the House'. The daughter of Sikh immigrants from India and identifying as queer, she says her interest in ______________ issues began much earlier when she was a teenager. She joined a ______________ – Labour – in 2013, and she helped the party in the Brexit ______________ in 2016. Her ______________ in the 'Remain' ______________ and the loss made her interested in becoming a ______________ herself. Following her ______________, she took a ______________ against the government's ______________ on unemployment and social issues, ______________ how unfair they were and does her part by ______________ half of her salary to local good ______________. Whittome is passionate and ______________ and she never ______________ saying what she thinks. When she isn't in the UK's ______________ for meetings at ______________, she lives and works part-time as a carer in Nottingham.

## 20 ACCESS TO WORDS Refining your presentation techniques

→ SB (p. 52) • SMC 30 (p. 73)

a) Write in the letter a–g for the best ending for 1–7 to make lines from a presentation. Then write in 'O' if it is a strong opening or 'E' for an ending with a bang.

1 ☐ 2 ☐ 3 ☐ 4 ☐ 5 ☐ 6 ☐ 7 ☐

☐ **1** In the time it takes me to say this one sentence,

☐ **2** I'll leave you with an appeal inspired by Gandhi: Be the

☐ **3** How often do you think

☐ **4** An American president once said

☐ **5** If you remember one thing from this presentation,

☐ **6** I don't have a final slide, I have

☐ **7** At the very start, let me say that we have something in common –

**a** you don't know what I'm going to say and neither do I!

**b** only this mirror: Look into it. The answers are there.

**c** remember this: ...

**d** about how far the food you eat has travelled to reach your mouth?

**e** change you want to see in the world.

**f** an area of rainforest equal to our school grounds has just been cut down.

**g** "A nation that destroys its forests destroys itself."

b) Match two boxes to make a presentation tip. Write the tips in your exercise book.

Presentation tips

5/21 Practise as often as you can.

...

**1** make eye · **2** opener · **3** early · **4** end with · **5** practise as often · **6** practise as often · **7** a script · **8** use a strong · **9** don't read out · **10** arrive · **11** don't speak · **12** your audience · **13** test all · **14** notes · **15** a bang · **16** keep it · **17** use · **18** audience · **19** equipment · **20** contact · **21** as you can · **22** too fast · **23** face your · **24** simple

## 1 We do need to take action (Emphatic *do* and other forms of emphasis)

Rewrite each sentence four times, adding emphasis in a different way each time.

1 Young people need to start campaigning.

2 My MP gets involved in local projects.

## 2 *Boxes of Hope*: a community project (Gerund after prepositions)

be · bring · do · feel · give · make · receive · start

Complete the text with the correct preposition and the gerund of a verb in the box.

*Boxes of Hope Cardiff* is a community project that was set up by Bev Jones in 2019. She was tired (1) ________ sad about children in Cardiff whose parents didn't have any money for Christmas presents, and she had the idea (2) ________ something to help. Bev told her friends that she was thinking (3) ________ her own initiative, and many of them were interested (4) ________ part of it. They bought presents that they thought young children would be keen (5) ________ – mainly toys, books and sweets. The gifts were packed into boxes and given to parents as a way (6) ________ sure that they had something to give their children on Christmas Day. "I believe (7) ________ the gift of hope at Christmas," explains Bev, who works on the project all year round. She says she dreams (8) ________ the initiative to all regions of Wales in the future.

## 3 The European Parliament in Brussels

a) Your class is planning a trip to Belgium. You are looking for information about visiting the European Parliament in Brussels. You find these pages on English-language websites. Skim the three texts. Mark the text in which you might find the information you need.

b) Scan the texts to find the answers to these two questions (underline the parts):

1 How can you watch the European Parliament's public meetings?
2 Do you need to buy tickets for the Parlamentarium before your visit?

**1** Would you like to learn more about public events at the European Parliament? The Parliament regularly organizes events that are of interest to members of the public. You can watch all public events online via live streaming, in real time. They include plenaries and committee meetings, plus special events like press conferences. When interpretation is available, you can listen to the broadcast in all the EU's official languages. To find out more, visit the European Parliament information office in your country or go to its website.

**2** No trip to Strasbourg would be complete without a visit to the European Parliament. The Parliament's Information Office in France organises guided tours whenever there is no plenary session running in Strasbourg. You'll be given a look into several different areas of the modern parliament building, including the famous meeting chamber. Tours are usually available in French, German or English. They are open to anyone aged 14 or over.

**3** The Parlamentarium is the European Parliament's visitor centre: the place to go to find out all about the Parliament, its history and how it works. Located in the Parliament's Espace Leopold complex in Brussels, the centre brings together exhibits, photos and videos that explain the Parliament and the other institutions of the European Union in an engaging way. Visits are suitable for school groups, families and individuals – and they don't cost a cent. There's no need to book in advance or even bring your ID card.

## 4 *Step Inside:* helping people back into the community

a) Scan the text and answer questions 1–6. Use your own words if possible. Write complete sentences in your exercise book. First mark keywords.

1 What is different about the clothes sold in the shop?
2 Why was it a good idea to start a shop?
3 What is the shop's location like?
4 What was the advantage for the students who helped Phil?
5 How many people has the charity helped get back into work this year?
6 Why do people in the area like the shop?

The new Step Inside boutique in Greenside Avenue might look like any other high-end clothes store, but there's one key difference: all the store's products are used. Step Inside was the brainchild of Phil Owens, a volunteer who works with local homeless charity The Dale Centre, which gives people forced to sleep rough a bed for the night during the freezing winter months. "*The Dale Centre* regularly receives donations of second-hand clothes and other items, and we can't always use all of them, so starting a shop seemed like the obvious solution," explains Phil. He found an empty shop in Greenside Avenue. "It's such a beautiful area with lovely shops, and I wanted ours to fit in with the others, so I decided to make it really smart. I asked a few local art students to get involved, and they did a marvellous job. When they'd finished, it looked like a designer store! It was the best thing we could have done, because by making it look great, we attracted large numbers of customers when we opened last month."

The students benefited too, adds Phil: "They had taken photos while working on the shop, and I said it would make a good project. So they told their college about it, and in the end, they were allowed to use the photos for their end-of-year design project. And they got top marks!"

The shop is run by a team of volunteers, and every penny it makes is invested in the work of *The Dale Centre*, which has already helped over 2,200 people to find a new home this year and almost 800 to find a job again. "The great thing about the shop is that we can also offer part-time volunteer positions to homeless people who need work experience or want to get back into the world of work," adds Phil. "And we give them clothes for job interviews. Local residents have told us how pleased they are, too, because they now have somewhere nearby where they can take their preloved clothes, and they feel good knowing that they're supporting a good cause."

b) What do the underlined words mean? Write the translations in your exercise book.

c) Explain what the *Step Inside* project does in your own words. Write about 50–100 words in your exercise book.

d) Would you buy used clothes from this shop or a similar one? Why (not)? Write about 50 words in your exercise book.

## Check: Reading

a) Vergleiche deine Antworten mit den Lösungen auf Seite 87 im Workbook.
b) Schätze deine Antworten mit einem grünen oder roten Gesicht ein.

| | ☺ | ☹ | |
|---|---|---|---|
| 1 Konntest du in Aufgabe 3 *skimmen* und dadurch den richtigen Text finden? | ○ | ○ | ➔ 1a |
| 2 Konntest du in Aufgabe 3 *scannen* und dadurch in b) schnell die richtigen Antworten finden? | ○ | ○ | ➔ 2a |
| 3 Konntest du in Aufgabe 4 wichtige *keywords/phrases* im Text erkennen und markieren? | ○ | ○ | ➔ 2a |
| 4 Konntest du in Aufgabe 4 mit Hilfe deiner *keywords* die Fragen richtig beantworten? | ○ | ○ | ➔ 2a |
| 5 Konntest du in 4b) die Wörter leicht erschließen oder im Wörterbuch schnell finden? | ○ | ○ | ➔ 1b |
| 6 Konntest du in 4c) die wichtigsten Informationen des Textes entnehmen und schriftlich zusammenfassen? | ○ | ○ | ➔ 1d |

c) Wenn du dich rot eingeschätzt hast, schau dir die rechte Spalte an. Die Nummern führen dich zu den passenden Übungen im Skills Training (S. 34–35). Dort kannst du gezielt Reading trainieren.

## 1 Recommended by bloggers ➜ *SMC 1, 2, 16 (pp. 60, 66)*

a) Skim the texts. What is the blog about? Circle A, B or C.

**TIP:** You skim the text to find out the main information. You scan to find details in part of the text with the help of keywords.

**A** Easter gifts **B** Lifestyle tips for vegans **C** Fashion and make-up

We never wear leather. That used to mean no alternatives except for ugly plastic fabrics. But now that the vegan community has become bigger and more mainstream, designers of clothes, shoes and accessories are using all kinds of weird and wonderful materials to create synthetic leather products that look and feel more natural. As the new Spring/ Summer season is about to start, we've been looking at some of the latest innovations. From amazing pineapple-leather sneakers to trendy shoulder bags made of paper to beautiful sandals made from 'ocean leather' (that's seaweed to you and me), there are plenty of better alternatives coming onto the market now. As well as being vegan – which is obviously our main concern – they're also much better for the environment. The animal-leather processing industry produces a lot of waste and pollution, but these new fabrics are all plant-based – just like our food. We've put together a shopping guide, just in time for the Easter holidays …

Hoping to receive some make-up, creams or other beauty products as an Easter gift? Just make sure they're safe as well as cruelty-free.

Make-up and other beauty treatments have been used for thousands of years, but in the past few hundred years, in particular, they have contained dangerous cocktails of chemicals. Did you know that in 1760 an Irish countess who died prematurely – aged just 27 – was described as a 'victim of cosmetics'? She wore make-up full of toxic chemicals, which got into her blood and killed her. Luckily, today's women (and men!) can easily find natural creams, lotions, gels, etc. that make them look good without damaging their health. Best of all, in our opinion, they are often vegan. So, if you'd like your Easter treats to include honey-free, milk-free beauty products that are safe and aren't tested on animals, this is what we recommend…

This week, we've been testing five of the best Easter lunch options to make sure that animal-lovers don't have to eat boring food during the holidays. From nut roast to glazed roast vegetables to sweet bunny cupcakes that are completely free from dairy products, we have plenty of recipe ideas for vegan Easter dishes. New recipes we've tried and loved include a tasty spinach quiche, a delicious cashew cheese lasagne and a mouth-watering pecan and mushroom Wellington. It seems that meat-free, dairy-free treats are trendy this spring, and we're certainly not complaining. Who says Easter has to be tough for the vegan community?

b) Mark these words in the text. Then find the correct German translations. Write in your exercise book.

1 accessories
2 concern
3 plant-based
4 glazed
5 bunny
6 mouth-watering
7 beauty products
8 cruelty-free
9 prematurely

**TIP:** Before you use a dictionary, consider the context, whether you know a similar word in English, German, French, Latin or any other languages, and whether there are clues in the pictures. If you do use a dictionary, choose the meaning that best fits the context.

c) In your exercise book, list the things found in food and beauty products that the blog's authors want to avoid.

d) Summarize each text in one sentence in your exercise book.

## 2 A book review: *Chocky* ➜ SMC 1, 4 (pp. 60, 61)

a) First read the questions and mark important words.
Then scan the text for the answers.
Write short answers in your exercise book.
Use your own words where possible.

**TIP:** Mark the keywords in the questions and look for them or similar words when you scan. Then read around the keywords to find the answers. Remember to look for different words or phrases with the same meaning.

1 What do Mr and Mrs Gore think about the situation with Chocky at first?

2 What basic things does Matthew tell his friend about?

3 What does Chocky hope to do?

4 Name two things that Matthew is now able to do well.

5 What makes the book different to others of the same genre?

6 Name one thing the writer of the review doesn't like about the novel.

**An engaging page-turner with an important message**

*Chocky* by John Wyndham is a short novel published in 1968. It tells the unusual story of 12-year-old Matthew Gore, who has a friend that only he can see. At first, his parents think he is a little old to behave like this, but they don't see any reason to do anything. However, they start to worry after hearing Matthew's conversations with his friend in which he explains that a week has seven days and the human race has males and females. At school, Matthew starts asking strange questions in maths lessons, and suddenly gets the best marks in science. He explains to his worried parents that this friend, Chocky, is a super-intelligent alien being who has come to Earth from a distant planet to learn about how everything works, with the hope of helping humans to improve the way they live and look after the planet that they call home.

Mr and Mrs Gore find it difficult to believe their son's explanation, but all the signs are there: Matthew saves his sister from drowning even though he has never been a good swimmer, and he wins prizes for painting even though he had never been good at art before. It appears that he is receiving help. His parents decide they need a medical opinion, and a visit to a psychiatrist confirms that the boy does seem to be in communication with something. Could it be that Chocky isn't just inside his head? The government is informed about the situation, and then things start to become dangerous for Matthew and his family.

Wyndham wrote several other famous works of science fiction, including *Day of the Triffids*, but compared with them – and most other novels from this genre – this is a very heart-warming book, even though the story might seem creepy at first. Both the way in which Mr Gore shows that he cares about his son and his gentle attitude towards the situation are lovely. And Chocky is not what you would expect from an alien visitor: she (Matthew says that on Chocky's planet there are no sexes, but Chocky sounds more like a 'she') is kind and is also worried about Matthew's safety, which is why she leaves at the end of the book.

The novel is forward-looking in the way that it raises questions about our terrible attitude towards the environment and the way we consume energy, as well as the corruption in our governments and societies. Being a 1960s novel, the gender roles described by Wyndham – as well as some of the characters' ways of speaking – seem rather old-fashioned now, but this was my only problem with the book. All in all, this is a gripping and thought-provoking read whose message is still relevant, given the way many people are unthinkingly destroying our amazing, beautiful planet.

b) Read the text in detail, then look at the guidelines for writing book reviews on pp. 41–43 of your student's book. Did this writer follow all the guidelines? Write 100–150 words in your exercise book explaining what you would improve.

c) Would you like to read the novel? Why (not)? Write 100–150 words in your exercise book.

### Part one: How to approach a reading exam

**Step 1:** Read the text closely. Do not let unknown words block you at this stage. Get a general understanding of the text. (➔ *SMC 1, p. 60*)

**Step 2:** Read the tasks carefully to understand what you need to find in the text. Highlight key words in the tasks and use them to help you mark important parts of the text so that you can find them again. (➔ *SMC 2, p. 60*)

**Step 3:** Now answer each question. If you have problems with a question, move on to the next, but do not forget to go back to it before you finish.

### Part two: An overview of reading tasks

In this section, you will practise the types of tasks you can expect in a reading exam.

## 1 Closed format tasks: Multiple choice and true or false

Tick (✓) the correct box and give evidence from the text by quoting short passages.

**How the Māori concept of *tauutuutu* can help Kiwi businesses** *By Erica Henry, business correspondent*

At the Wellington Business Forum today, Professor Eileen Jones gave a presentation on how New Zealand's businesses can benefit from learning about Māori customs and beliefs. She focused on *tauutuutu*, a Māori word that has no direct equivalent in the English language but in simple terms means giving more than you receive to create good relationships with people and nature.

1 Professor Jones talked about how firms in the country should educate themselves about indigenous …

**A** ☐ languages. **B** ☐ traditions. **C** ☐ consumers.

**TIP:** Write clearly – if your answer cannot be read, you will lose marks.

Evidence: ______________________________

______________________________

2 *Tauutuutu* can be easily translated into English.

This statement is … ☐ true ☐ false

Evidence: ______________________________

## 2 Closed format tasks: Matching

Read the text and match the feedback to the people who gave it. Write in the people's names in the table. There is one more question than you need.

**Reviews of Waitangi Treaty Grounds**

**Bella:** "We'll never forget our visit. We learned so much and all of the staff were so friendly. My family found the hāngi meal delicious, though it would've been nice if they'd had a vegan option."

**Joe:** "The live performances were out of this world, from the inspiring powhiri with its beautiful chanting that greeted us to the traditional haka at the end. I can imagine how enemies in the past must've been terrified. Take note: my guide dog was allowed, but other animals aren't – kiwi birds roam free there."

**Kiruba:** "I can't recommend it more highly. I think the "Price of Citizenship" exhibition was the most moving part. It really opened my eyes to how badly society has treated the Māori."

| Who says … | | Name |
|---|---|---|
| 1 | … you can learn about discrimination in New Zealand? | ____________ |
| 2 | … that pets are not permitted in the attraction? | ____________ |
| 3 | … that visitors are welcomed with a musical ceremony? | ____________ |
| 4 | … the kiwi exhibition doesn't cost anything? | ____________ |
| 5 | … only dishes with animal products are served? | ____________ |

**TIP:** Sometimes not all the answers are stated directly in the text, and you have to 'read between the lines'.

## 3 Semi-open format tasks: Fill in

**Complete the sentences about Emily's blog post.**

www.emilysdesk.blogspot.co.uk/may/2305.htm

I have to say I'm angry. Yesterday, I saw someone complaining on social media about public information being printed in Polish. "We speak English in this country," they said. It just shows how little they know. Britain has a long and rich heritage as a multilingual society. Did you know that there are over 10 indigenous languages spoken in the UK nowadays besides English? And the majority are ancient compared to English. There are worries that these languages are dying but the latest statistics for Wales, for example, show that the percentage of the population who can chat in Welsh has remained steady, although the figure for daily speakers has gone down slightly.

1 Most native languages spoken in Britain are a lot ____________ English.

2 The number of people who can have a conversation in Welsh ____________

____________ recently.

**TIP:** If a question refers to amounts or begins with 'How much/many', scan the text for numbers.

## 4 Semi-open format tasks: Short answers

**Read the extract from *The Whale Rider*. Write short answers to the questions that follow the text.**

Two weeks after the school break-up ceremony, Koro Apirana took the young boys from the school onto the sea. It was early morning as he put them in his boat and headed out past the bay where the water suddenly turned dark green.
When the sun tipped the sea, Koro Apirana began a prayer. He had a carved stone in his hand and suddenly he threw it into the ocean. The boys watched until they could see it no longer. 'One of you must bring that stone back to me,' Koro Apirana said. 'Go now.'
The boys were eager to prove themselves, but the stone had gone too deep. Some were afraid of the darkness. Others were unable to dive so far down. Despite valiant attempts they could not do it.
Koro Apirana's face sagged. 'Okay, boys, you've done well. Let's get you all home.'
When he got back home, Koro Apirana shut himself in the bedroom. Slowly, he began to lament.

1 Why does Koro Apirana take the group of boys on a boat trip?

____________

2 Describe Koro Apirana's feelings as he returns to his house.

____________

Part three: Mixed practice

## 5 Tongariro National Park

Read the article below about one of New Zealand's most popular tourist attractions and answer the questions. Write your answers in your exercise book. For questions 1–3, 5 and 7, give evidence from the text for your answers.

### Tongariro National Park

**A** In Māori tradition, mountains were once gods and fearsome warriors and when you see the sometimes fiery peaks of Tongariro National Park, it is easy to understand why. You don't need to worry about lava too much though – the last eruption was around fifteen years ago!

**B** Mount Tongariro and its neighbours, Ngāuruhoe and Ruapehu, are awe-inspiring. No wonder then, that on some days the warmly dressed tourists winding their way through the Tongariro Alpine Crossing form an unbroken line.

**C** The Māori name for the three volcanoes, Te Kāhui Tupua, translates to "the sacred peaks", while their northern neighbour Lake Taupā, New Zealand's largest lake, is considered the heart of Aotearoa/New Zealand's North Island. If you draw a line north through the three peaks, you will find the mountain of Pihanga, covered in deep green forest. The Māori people of the region respect this mountain as sacred and feminine. Indeed, it is said that a fourth mountain, Taranaki, once stood in the same area and that the four male mountains adored Pihanga so much that they battled with each other to win her affections. Tongariro ultimately triumphed and earned the right to stay by Pihanga's side, becoming the supreme leader of the land.

**D** It was thanks to the warriors' attacks with hot boulders and streams of molten lava that the area around the three mountains was left barren and cratered yet spectacularly gorgeous, as any tourist fit enough to scale the heights of the park can tell you. The Whanganui River is yet another sign of the legendary struggle: the defeated Taranaki was forced to leave, angrily tearing the land and forming the river valley as he stomped west to the coast.

**E** The Māori guardians of the area, the Ngāti Tāwharetoa, came to an arrangement with the Crown authorities in the late 19th century which meant the peaks of the mountains could never be sold. Thus the area became the first ever national park created by a gift from indigenous people. Now recognised as a double World Heritage site for its outstanding natural and cultural aspects, a visit to the park is a must-do for tourists and New Zealanders alike.

1 The park's volcanoes have not been active since around the year 1900. Is this statement true or false? ____________

2 Occasionally, there are so many tourists visiting the mountains that …

**A** ☐ the path is very full. **B** ☐ the waiting times are long. **C** ☐ the park stops more from coming.

3 Legend says that the gods fought over the love of Pihanga. Is this statement true or false? ____________

4 It was as a result of his ______________________________ that Tongariro remains close to Pihanga today.

5 The landscape around the sacred peaks is …

**A** ☐ fertile and very lovely. **B** ☐ quite rocky and even scary. **C** ☐ empty but very beautiful.

6 The British government and the local Māori tribe ______________________________ to protect and keep the land for all the people of New Zealand.

7 In which of the sections A–E can you find the answers to these questions?
There is one more question than you need.

| | | | |
|---|---|---|---|
| **1** When was the park founded? | ☐ | **4** Should I expect some physical exercise on a visit? | ☐ |
| **2** What should I wear when I go there? | ☐ | **5** Should I be concerned about the volcanoes? | ☐ |
| **3** How far from the coast is the park? | ☐ | **6** On which part of New Zealand is the park located? | ☐ |

An overview of vocabulary tasks

## 1 Multiple choice

First, read questions 1–4 and the possible answers. If you are sure of an answer, tick (✓) the correct box. If not, follow steps 1–4.

**Step 1:** Read the sentence carefully. Highlight the verbs and important nouns.
**Step 2:** Look at the possible answers. Ask yourself if any of them form common collocations with the key words in the sentence.
**Step 3:** Try saying the sentence with each possible answer in the gap.
**Step 4:** Make a choice and move on to the next question.

1 European countries are considering following Britain's example of ... school uniforms, to reduce the stress children feel about choosing what to wear.

**A** ☐ necessity **B** ☐ compulsory **C** ☐ optional **D** ☐ voluntary

2 Despite the end of the pandemic, school ... is at a lower level, with parents keeping children at home because of minor health issues such as colds, etc.

**A** ☐ absence **B** ☐ truancy **C** ☐ attendance **D** ☐ participate

3 Despite their youth, students make serious decisions which ... the rest of their lives.

**A** ☐ affect **B** ☐ choose **C** ☐ alternate **D** ☐ effect

4 Some experts question the value of ... exams as a form of preparation for adult life.

**A** ☐ making **B** ☐ performing **C** ☐ doing **D** ☐ writing

**TIP:** At the beginning of the school year, keep a vocabulary notebook. When you record new words, use
- word families,
- example sentences,
- common collocations

to help you really learn them. (➜ *SMC 39, p. 76*)

**TIP:** Be careful of false friends and the influence of your own language. When you read the sentences, say them to yourself in English – do not translate.

## 2 Fill in

In this type of task, you need to make sure that your answer fits the sentence in terms of meaning and grammatical form.

a) Before you do questions 1–5, read them carefully and write in the number of the question beside the type of word which is needed in the answer. The first is done for you.

Verb (2 x): ________ Adjective (1 x): *1* ________ Noun (2 x): ________

b) Now fill in suitable words.

1 Tourism can generate much needed income for ____________ communities, such as the Māori in New Zealand, which may have suffered from economic and social disadvantages.

2 For the Māori, tourism can raise ____________ of their culture, values and history in wider society.

3 However, some Māori people believe the ____________ of mass tourism on their culture and sacred sites outweighs its economic benefits.

4 The behaviour of some tourists, in search of the perfect selfie for example, risks causing offence or even physical damage to the sites which are ____________ sacred.

5 Some in the Māori community worry that presenting rituals like the haka ceremonial dance or powhiri welcome ritual as tourist attractions ____________ superficial stereotypes of Māori culture.

**TIP:** Pay close attention to the words on both sides of the gap. For example: if there is a preposition immediately before a gap and a verb is needed, you need the *-ing* verb form. Some (phrasal) verbs and nouns need certain prepositions – look for prepositions on the right side of the gap.

# How is the world changing?

## 1 Past, present, future ➔ *SB (pp. 56–57) • SMC 32 (p. 74)*

Use the pictures to think about how technology will affect shopping in the future. Make notes and discuss with a partner the advantages and disadvantages of online shopping.
What might happen if we all ordered everything for delivery by drone?

*Photo 1 shows ... Picture 2 shows ...*
*The advantages/disadvantages are ...*
*If everything were delivered by drone, we would ...*

1

2

## 2 Your world – your future ➔ *SB (p. 57) • SMC 26 (p. 71)*

a) 20 Listen to the first part of a conversation between Emily and her dad, Colin. Circle the correct answer. You can listen twice.

1 Emily says her dad is constantly on his phone ...
- **A** checking the news.
- **B** messaging his work colleagues.
- **C** talking to his latest girlfriend.

2 On his most recent date, Colin didn't like that ...
- **A** Mary was not a pet lover.
- **B** Mary's online profile was not accurate.
- **C** Mary was still married.

3 Emily's parents went out on their first date ...
- **A** after they had been friends for a long time.
- **B** without knowing each other before.
- **C** after Emily's mum asked Colin.

4 Emily's friends use dating apps but they ...
- **A** take their personal safety seriously.
- **B** never tell their friends who they are dating.
- **C** don't use them safely.

b) 21 Listen to the second part of Colin's and Emily's conversation. Complete the statements below. Use as few words as possible. You can listen twice.

1 Colin has heard stories of strangers finding out about house parties because the host ...

______________________________________________

2 An older girl at Emily's school had a party where there was a lot of damage and the girl's father ...

______________________________________________

3 Colin says that posting a lot of party photos online when you are younger can cause problems later because ...

______________________________________________

## 3 WORDS Robo-journalism ➔ SB (pp. 58–59)

Complete the text with words from the box in the correct form. You will not need all the words.

although · *artificial* · attraction · browse · celebrity · however · disinformation · nevertheless · publish · see · sell · themselves · theory · use · write

Nowadays, the news is full of reports about *artificial* (1) intelligence (AI). This might be linked to the growing fear of journalists ________ (2) that their jobs could be among the first to be lost to AI. But automated or robo-journalism is not new – for years, companies ________ (3) 'robot'-written news content. Until now this content has taken the form of 'listicles', articles which are basically lists of sports results or top tourist ________ (4) in a region, for example. Relatively simple bots ________ (5) the internet for the relevant data and then package it into a news report ________ (6) the standard language of the genre. A major concern, ________ (7), is the accuracy of this content. After all, the data which the bots find may or may not be true and bots have been used in the past to spread ________ (8) such as fake news or conspiracy ________ (9) on social media. ________ (10), as the language skills of AI-programs improve, in the near future we ________ (11) increasing quantities and different kinds of AI-authored content in our news media. In fact, in March 2023, two major UK tabloid newspapers ________ (12) their first articles ________ (13) using AI. The future is here, it seems.

## 4 REVISION What might happen in the future (The definite article) ➔ SB (p. 60)

a) Look at p. 156 of your student's book and read about the use of the definite article in English. Then look at the following words and tick (✓) where the definite article is needed.

1 ☐ science
2 ☐ dictionary
3 ☐ living in a city
4 ☐ most of the students
5 ☐ Greek food
6 ☐ future

b) Decide where you need to add a definite article to the sentences below.

1 I believe ________ people will be replaced by ________ robots in many jobs in the future.

2 ________ technological progress we have seen over the last few years has been extremely fast.

3 ________ unemployment[1] will grow because ________ computers will do our jobs.

4 Almost every computer on ________ planet is connected to ________ internet nowadays.

5 In my school, everyone thinks ________ packages will be delivered by ________ drones in ________ future.

6 ________ most crops[2] need ________ bees to help pollinate[3] them.

7 What can we do to help ________ insects that are having problems surviving ________ climate change?

[1]unemployment [ˌʌnɪm'plɔɪmənt] *Arbeitslosigkeit* [2]crop ['krɒp] *(Feld-)Frucht* [3]pollinate ['pɒləneɪt] *bestäuben*

## 5 REVISION The web never forgets (Sequence of adverbials) ➜ SB (p. 60)

Rewrite the sentences including the adverbials.

1 Think before posting something embarrassing on social media. (carefully, potentially[1])

2 There have been cases of young people posting videos of bullying. (lately, on the web)

3 A 13-year-old girl from North Wales became upset after someone uploaded a video. (extremely, in September 2021)

4 Only classmates saw it, but it went viral. (at first, quickly)

5 Arriving at school, they found two police officers waiting in the classroom. (patiently, the next morning)

6 The girl's mother had become so angry that she reported the class to the police. (the night before, immediately)

7 The police decided that there wasn't enough evidence[2]. (in the end, really)

8 The school decided to take action and punished the whole class. (finally, instead)

9 We will find out who uploaded the video. (probably, to the web, unfortunately, never)

[1]potentially [pə'tenʃəli] möglicherweise [2]evidence ['evɪdəns] Beweis

b) ● Arrange the following sentences containing adverbs in the right order and highlight the adverbs.

1 almost · a mobile phone · Today · and upload · and can take · everyone has · to the internet · images

2 with that · we're doing · always · think · The danger · carefully · about what · is we don't

3 quickly · and millions of people · Photos can · we even realise · can see them · before · go viral

4 often · to check · It's important · and your photos are · are OK · that your settings · properly protected

5 to check · you still need · can see your messages · regularly · that only people you want · you're careful · Even if

6 so don't · just add everyone · become a big problem · Unfortunately · to a website · who invites you · cyber-bullying · has

7 immediately · delete it · If a friend · quickly · so they can · tell them · posts something they shouldn't

8 many problems · forever · but a photo · Luckily · can stay · are forgotten · in the cyberworld · quickly

c) Imagine you are giving advice to younger students about joining a new social media site. Think of what's important to remember when giving out personal information. Write a paragraph giving at least five internet safety tips in your exercise book. Use a variety of different adverbs and the following words or your own words.

be careful · check if · don't meet · never give out · your address

## 6 ACCESS TO WORDS Staying connected ➜ SB (p. 61)

a) What can you do in the following situations? Use a verb from box **A** and a suitable noun (or phrase) from box **B** and write the collocations below. There may be several correct options.

**A**

block · browse · charge · click on · customize · delete · enter · export · increase · manage · open · press · replace · swipe

**B**

a new tab · a phrase in the search bar · the attachment · the battery · the button · the icon · the web · to a different format · unwanted friend requests · your card · your computer's memory · your contact list · your phone · your settings

______ ______ ______

______ ______ ______

______ ______ ______

______ ______ ______

______ ______

b) Now go through the collocations from a) and write ten or more sentences using them.

1 *If some programs start to run slowly, you can increase your computer's memory.*

______

______

______

______

______

______

______

______

______

## 7 Feature article ➜ SB (pp. 63–65) • SMC 1–2 (p. 60)

a) How many different crops do you know? Make a mind map in your exercise book using *vegetable*, *fruit* and *grain* as umbrella words.

b) Read the text, add ideas to your mind map and sum up its message in two sentences.

### SOS – Save our seeds!

**No matter where you go, every supermarket seems to have the same fruit and vegetables. Go to the market and you might find a bit more variety, but it still won't come close to the range of different foods the older generation used to enjoy. Maybe some of your grandparents' favourite childhood foods don't even exist any more.**

Vegetables, just like clothes, go in and out of fashion. Until not long ago, people would grow their own food in the garden, and they would carefully plant and harvest their own 'mini' crops all year round. Because of our hectic and urban lifestyles, people just aren't producing their own vegetables any more, and the farmers who put food on our tables are turning to higher-yield[1] crops to maximize profit. A 1999 study carried out by the UN's Food and Agriculture Organization (FAO) revealed that over the last century, 75 % of agricultural crops had been lost. The result is that today, 75 % of the world's food is limited to just 12 species of plant. When people don't grow crops, the seeds become worthless.

Scientists who were horrified by the idea of losing this diversity started discussions in the 1980s about what could be done. The result was the opening, in 2008, of the Svalbard Global Seed Vault[2] on the Norwegian island of Spitsbergen located in the Arctic Ocean. The idea was to set up a permanent 'library' holding a backup copy of seeds stored in different gene banks all over the world. In the event of war, bad management or something as simple as a broken freezer, there would be a duplicate in Norway so that there is always a surviving seed somewhere on the planet.

Since opening a decade ago, over 5,000 species and 890,000 seed samples have been brought to the island. The Vault itself can hold over 4.5 million seed samples, and each sample can contain an average of 500 seeds, so there is still plenty of room available.

Lots of different governments and research centres work closely with the Norwegian Ministry of Agriculture and Food, the Nordic Genetic Resource Centre (NordGen) and the Crop Trust in Germany, which run the facility, to store seeds for future generations. They do this in the Vault, which is housed in a mountain and which remains at a constant −18° Celsius. Because it is so cold deep in the mountain, even if the electricity failed or there was a problem with the Vault's systems, the seeds would stay frozen long enough to be saved. Norway's political stability will also help make sure the seeds are protected for years to come.

In an ideal world, the seeds we lock safely away in the freezing Vault will never be needed. However, one country has unfortunately already had to withdraw[3] some samples. With the escalation of conflict in Aleppo, ICARDA (The International Centre for Agricultural Research in Dry Areas) had to evacuate its Syrian office, which meant the loss of an important local resource. Luckily, they had stored a backup of nearly all their seeds in the vault in Norway. Without it, some crops may have been lost forever.

We can never be sure what is going to happen in our world, and nutritionists and scientists believe it is vital we start planning for the future now. The Global Seed Vault truly is a way to Save Our Seeds!

c) ○ Identify where you can find the different parts of the structure.

Headline l./ll. ______ Introduction l./ll. ______ Conclusion l./ll. ______

Summary l./ll. ______ Main body l./ll. ______

[1]yield [ji:ld] *Ertrag* [2]vault [vɔ:lt] *Tresor* [3]withdraw [wɪð'drɔ:] hier: *entnehmen*

d) Look at these statements about the text. Tick (✓) the correct box and give evidence from the article.

1 In the past, when buying fruit and vegetables, consumers could choose from ...

**A** ☐ a narrower range. **B** ☐ the same range as today. **C** ☐ a broader range.

**Evidence:** ______________________________

______________________________

2 People don't grow their own food nowadays because ...

**A** ☐ they live in towns and are too busy. **B** ☐ it is not trendy. **C** ☐ farmers are selling food more cheaply.

**Evidence:** ______________________________

______________________________

3 By the end of the 20th century, the number of different food plants grown by humans ...

**A** ☐ had fallen by a quarter. **B** ☐ was a quarter of what it had been. **C** ☐ had risen by three-quarters.

**Evidence:** ______________________________

______________________________

4 Ten years since it began operation, the Seed Vault ...

**A** ☐ was under 25 % full. **B** ☐ held over four million seed samples. **C** ☐ had very little space left.

**Evidence:** ______________________________

______________________________

5 Fortunately, there hasn't been any reason to use the seeds stored in the Svalbard Seed Vault so far.

This statement is ☐ true ☐ false

**Evidence:** ______________________________

______________________________

e) ● Find the following nouns or noun phrases in the text and match the phrases they are followed by to the terms in the box. Write the terms in the right column.

contact clause · defining relative clause · relative clause with "which" · non-defining relative clause

ll. 5–6: range of different foods ______________________________ __________

l. 23: Scientists ______________________________ __________

______________________________ __________

l. 43: Crop Trust in Germany, ______________________________ __________

______________________________ __________

l. 59: Syrian office, ______________________________ __________

______________________________ __________

f) Add a relative clause to give some extra information on each of the following sentences. Use your own ideas.

1 Our lives are very hectic nowadays. *Our lives are very hectic nowadays, which leaves no time for our families and friends.*

2 Farmers now only grow 12 different species of plant. ______

3 A permanent 'library' of seeds will be stored inside an Arctic mountain. ______

4 The Vault can hold over 4.5 million samples. ______

5 These samples are kept at a constant temperature of –18° Celsius. ______

6 Norway is a very stable democracy. ______

7 The headquarters of ICARDA in Aleppo were damaged. ______

8 We cannot guarantee[1] the safety of seeds in times of war or natural disaster. ______

## 8 EXTRA Keeping the planet safe

➔ *SB (p. 67) • SMC30 (p. 73) • Wordbank 4, 5*

● What do you know about different types of renewable[2] energy?

a) Choose one of the following technologies and present its advantages and disadvantages. Use the internet to research information and make notes.

**TIP:** These words will help with your research: *wind farm, solar panel, biomass, biodiesel, (wood) pellets, offshore/onshore*

b) Working in small groups, present your findings to one another.

c) Hold a class vote on which technology is the most interesting and promising.

[1]guarantee sth. [ˌgærən'tiː] etwas garantieren [2]renewable [rɪ'njuːəbl] [3]turbine ['tɜːbaɪn]

## 9 STUDY SKILLS Analysing a text – Part 2 ➜ SB (p. 71)

a) Read this excerpt from the third chapter of the novel *About a Boy* by Nick Hornby. The novel tells the fictional story of the unusual friendship which develops between Marcus, a young boy who has just moved to London with his mother, and Will, a rich and single thirty-six year old man. In the novel, before the excerpt you are about to read, Marcus has his first day at his new secondary school. When you have read the excerpt, do tasks b)–f) on the next page.

### Chapter Three

During the night after his first day **(1)** Marcus woke up every half-hour or so. He could tell from the luminous[1] hands of **(2)** his dinosaur clock: 10.41, 11.19, 11.55, 12.35, 12.55, 1.31 … He couldn't believe he was going to have to go back there the next morning, and the morning after that, and the morning after that, and … well, then it would be the weekend, but more or less every morning for the rest of his life, just about. […]

**(3)** All that night he thought like boomerangs fly: an idea would shoot way off into the distance, all the way to a caravan in Hollywood and, for a moment, when he had got as far away from school and reality as it was possible to go, he was reasonably[2] happy; then it would begin the return journey, thump him on the head, and leave him in exactly the place he had started from. And all the time it got nearer and nearer to the morning. […]

He got to school early, went to the form room, sat down at his desk. He was safe enough there. **(4)** The kids who had given him a hard time yesterday were probably not the sort to arrive at school first thing; **(5)** they'd be off somewhere smoking and taking drugs and raping people. He thought darkly. There were a couple of girls in the room, but **(6)** they ignored him, unless the snort[3] of laughter he heard while he was getting his reading book out had anything to do with him.

What was there to laugh at? Not much, really, unless you were the kind of person who was on permanent lookout for something to laugh at. Unfortunately, **(7)** that was exactly the kind of person most kids were, in his experience. They patrolled up and down school corridors like sharks, except that what they were on the lookout for wasn't flesh but the wrong trousers, or the wrong haircut, or the wrong shoes, any or all of which sent them wild with excitement. […]

**(8)** [I]f you wanted to make people laugh at you, really, really laugh, then the best way, he had discovered, better even than to have a bad haircut, was to sing out loud when everybody else in the room was quiet and bored. […]

[T]hen in English things went bad again. They were using one of those books that had a bit of everything in them; the bit they were looking at was taken from *One Flew Over the Cuckoo's Nest*. He knew the story, because **(9)** he'd seen the film with his mum, and so he could see really clearly, so clearly that **(10)** he wanted to run from the room, what was going to happen.

When it happened it was even worse than he thought it was going to be. Ms Maguire got one of the girls who she knew was a good reader to read out the passage, and then she tried to get a discussion going.

'Now, one of the things this book is about is … How do we know who's mad[4] and who isn't? Because, you know, in a way we're all a bit mad, and if someone decides that we're a bit mad, how do we … how do we show them we're sane[5]?'

Silence. A couple of the kids sighed and rolled their eyes at each other. **(11)** One thing Marcus had noticed was that when you came into a school late you could tell straight away how well the teachers got on with a class. Ms Maguire was young and nervous and she was struggling, he reckoned[6]. This class could go either way.

'OK, let's put it another way. How can we tell if people are mad?'

Here it comes, he thought. Here it comes. This is it.

'If they sing for no reason in class, miss.'

Laughter. But then it all got worse than he'd expected. Everyone turned round and looked at him; he looked at Ms Maguire, but she had this big forced grin on and she wouldn't catch his eye.

'OK, that's one way of telling, yes. You'd think that someone who does that would be a little potty[7]. But leaving Marcus out of it for a moment …'

More laughter. **(12)** He knew what she was doing and why, and he hated her.

[1] luminous ['luːmɪnəs] *im Dunkeln leuchtend* [2] reasonably ['riːznəblɪ] *ziemlich* [3] snort [snɔːt] *Prusten* [4] mad [mæd] *verrückt* [5] sane [seɪn] *geistig gesund* [6] reckon ['rekən] *glauben* [7] potty ['pɒtɪ] *verrückt*

| | Jack  | Sara  | Marcus  |
|---|---|---|---|
| **Height** | Do you know Jack? He's pretty tall (for his age, at least). | I want to tell you about Sara. Her **height** is average, neither tall nor short, | Here's a photo of Marcus. He's a bit **on the short side**, |
| **Build** | He says he's **skinny**; I'd describe him as thin, about average build but not that **muscular**, it's true. | and she's quite athletic – **slim** and **toned**. | and kind of **stocky**. I wouldn't say fat or chubby, but definitely fairly **chunky** in a nice way, with |
| **Hair** | His hair is medium-length and **wavy** brown, but it used to be much longer. | The first thing you notice is her long blond dreadlocks, and **dyed** hair – bits of pink today! | short **frizzy** black hair and a short beard and **moustache** too. He's worried about going bald, but I think it's more that |
| **Face** | His face is long, with high **cheek-bones**, and you won't find a more | Sara says her face is **chubby**; I think it's round and **suits** her. Her ears are **pierced**, of course, and she's very | his **forehead** is high! There's always a smile on his face – you can't imagine anyone more **cheerful** and ready for a |
| **Character** | relaxed person. I think you'd like him. At times, Jack can be rather **vain**. For example, he has glasses, but **rarely** wears them. He can also be **disorganized**. On the other hand, people agree he's an easy-going sort of person who's also very hard-working. Everyone says Jack's the calm but confident type, though not always terribly reliable. | cool. Although she **gives the impression of** being very **outgoing**, she's in fact not that confident and once told me she often feels shy in company. It's true Sara's not always very talkative, but you'd never describe her as boring. There's a serious side to her too – she's a great reader. | laugh. At the same time, he's really creative and is into music and art in a big way. His **ambition** is to be a DJ, which is something he's very serious about. Marcus **comes across as** someone who's friendly and always ready to help. It's great to have him as a friend: I've found him to be patient and a really good listener. |
| **Clothes** | His style is smart casual – you know, jeans and T-shirts but I've seen him in a suit and he looked really good in it. | Her style in clothes shows her **sporty** nature: trainers and **tracksuit** bottoms are the norm. She **tends to** wear darker colours. That makes her hair **stand out** even more! | **In terms of** clothing, you're most likely to find him in loose and **baggy** clothes and not choosing a weird creative appearance, if you know what I mean. |

**Write a short description of a famous person or someone you know, but don't give the name. Can your partner guess who your person is?**

**TIP:** Be sensitive, polite and less direct than you might be if writing in German.
~~He's very fat.~~ He's a bit on the heavy side.
~~She is nervous.~~ She gives the impression of being nervous.

**Height:** height [haɪt] *(Körper)Größe* He's on the short/fat/… side. *Er ist eher klein/dick/…* **Build:** build *Körperbau* chunky *stämmig* muscular ['mʌskjələ] *muskulös* skinny *abgemagert* slim *schlank* stocky *pummelig* toned [təʊnd] *fit, stark* **Hair:** dyed [daɪd] *gefärbt* forehead ['fɔːhed, 'fɒrɪd] *Stirn* frizzy *kraus* moustache [mə'stɑːʃ] *Schnurrbart* wavy ['weɪvi] *wellig* **Face:** cheekbone ['tʃiːkbəʊn] *Wangenknochen* chubby *pausbäckig* pierced *durchlocht, gepierct* (to) suit sb. *jm. passen* **Character:** ambition [æm'bɪʃn] *Ambition, Ehrgeiz* cheerful ['tʃɪəfl] *heiter* (to) come across as sth. *als etwas wirken* disorganized [dɪs'ɔːgənaɪzd] *schlecht organisiert, chaotisch* (to) give the impression of doing sth. *den Eindruck machen/vermitteln, etwas zu tun* outgoing ['aʊtgəʊɪŋ] *aus sich herausgehend, extrovertiert* rarely ['reəli] *selten* vain [veɪn] *eitel* **Clothes:** baggy *ausgebeult* in terms of … *Was … angeht/betrifft* norm *Regel* sporty ['spɔːti] *sportlich, sportbegeistert* (to) stand out *auffallen* (to) tend to do sth. *dazu neigen, etwas zu tun* tracksuit bottoms *(pl)* ['træksuːt ˌbɒtəmz] *Jogginghose*

*Fotos:* Shutterstock (Jack: Milles Studio; Sara: PHB.cz (Richard Semik); Marcus: Akhenaton Images)

## 1 Making requests

## 2 Asking for information and help

battery *Akku* (to) charge *aufladen* autograph *Autogramm* I don't suppose you could … *Du könntest wohl nicht für mich …?*

## 3 Saying what you would and wouldn't like to do

**Making plans**

What I'd really love to **do** is see that new James Bond film. Do you want to come with me?

**Thanks for asking, but** I'm **not that keen** on action movies, actually. What about eating out?

**Another idea …**

**I wouldn't mind** trying that new Chinese restaurant.

**I'm not a big fan of** Chinese food, actually.

**Or …**

Actually, **I wouldn't mind** watching sport on TV for a while. What do you think?

**I'd rather not** do that, to be honest. **I'm not too fond of** watching TV in the day time.

**Or …**

**But I wouldn't mind** an afternoon in town. We could have a look in the shops and maybe get some new shoes.

**I would rather you didn't** take me to any more shoe shops, to be honest. How about going for a coffee somewhere?

**Or …**

A coffee would be wonderful. How about that place by the park? Or the new one in the shopping centre?

I don't have strong feelings either way.

## 4 Saying someone is wrong or mistaken

I'd rather … [ˈrɑːðə] *Ich würde lieber …* (to) be fond of sth. *etwas gerne haben* I would rather … *Ich möchte lieber …* idiot [ˈɪdiət] *Idiot/in* satellite [ˈsætəlaɪt] *Satellit* unmanned *unbesetzt* mission [ˈmɪʃn] *Mission* absolutely *unbedingt*

*Illustrationen:* Christian Bartz, Berlin

First, you have to be 18 or older, then you have to register in the **constituency** where you live. UK citizens have the right to vote, as well as Irish and Commonwealth citizens living in the UK. In England, there are elections to the House of Commons and local **councils**. Some cities also elect their police and crime **commissioners**.
The most important election is the General Election to the House of Commons, which by law has to take place every five years. Anybody can stand for election to parliament if they can make a £500 **deposit** and find 10 people to support them. Candidates who don't reach a 5% **threshold** don't get their deposit back.
**Polling** day is always on a Thursday. Voters either go to their local polling station, send a postal vote, or ask a friend to vote **by proxy**.
Polling stations are open from 7 am to 10 pm. You give your name to the people there (we have no ID cards here!), and your name is crossed off the list.
Then you go into a voting **booth** and mark the **ballot paper** with just one cross next to the name of the candidate you want to vote for. You then put the paper into the ballot box.
At 10 pm, the boxes are taken to a counting location in each constituency, often a sports hall, and the votes are counted. When this is over, the **Returning Officer** announces the winner.
The General Election uses a "first past the post" system, which means that only one candidate is elected as MP for the constituency. This often means that MPs are elected with less than 50% of the vote.
The party with the most MPs (out of 650) forms the new government.

ballot paper ['bælət] *Stimmzettel* booth [buːð] *Kabine* by proxy ['prɒksi] *mit Vollmacht* constituency [kən'stɪtjuənsi] *Wahlkreis* deposit [dɪ'pɒzɪt] *Pfand* police and crime commissioner [kə'mɪʃənə] ≈ *Polizeipräsident/in* polling ['pəʊlɪŋ] *Wählen, Wahl* Returning Officer *Wahlleiter/in* threshold ['θreʃhəʊld] *Hürde*

We Americans have to be 18 or over to vote, and we have to register first.
If you can't or don't want to go to the polling station on Election Day, you can vote via an **absentee ballot**, which you send by post. In some states you can choose "early voting": you go to the polling station before Election Day. 70% chose this option in the 2020 presidential election.
Voters usually **cast** their ballots with scanning machines (with a pen) or electronic machines (with buttons or a touchscreen).
Federal elections are for the House of Representatives (435 members elected for 2 years) and the Senate (100 members elected for 6 years).
The presidential election is different: each of the 50 states chooses **Electors**. States with larger populations have more Electors, smaller states fewer (California has 55, eight states have only 3). The members of the Electoral **College** vote for the presidential candidate who won the highest number of popular votes in their state. This "winner takes all" system means that a candidate can be elected president with fewer popular votes nationwide than their **opponent**. This has happened five times in US history: in 1824, 1876, 1888, 2000 and 2016.
There are also state elections (e. g. for governor) and local elections (e. g. at city level, for mayor and city councils).

absentee ballot [æbsən'tiː] *Briefwahl* (to) cast [kɑːst] *abgeben* college ['kɒlɪdʒ] *(Wahl)Kollegium* elector [ɪ'lektə] *Wahlmann, -frau* opponent [ə'pəʊnənt] *Gegner/in*

**Use these notes or your own experiences and write an explanation of the German electoral system.**

In der Bundesrepublik gibt es neben Wahlen zum Europäischen Parlament drei verschiedene Wahlen. Bei den Kommunalwahlen geht es um die niedrigste Ebene, also um die Gemeinde oder den Stadtbezirk. In jedem Bundesland gibt es ein unterschiedliches Wahlrecht. Die Landesparlamente haben verschiedene Namen. Hier werden MdL, MdA, MdBB bzw. MdHB gewählt. Mitglieder der jeweiligen Landesregierungen sind im Bundesrat vertreten.
Die Bundestagswahl findet alle vier Jahre statt. Zwei Besonderheiten sind in Deutschland wichtig: die Erst-/Zweitstimme und die Fünfprozenthürde. Die Erststimme geht an eine Person. Wer die meisten Stimmen bekommt, erhält ein Direktmandat und wird MdB seines Wahlkreises, von denen es zurzeit 299 gibt. Die Zweitstimme geht an eine Partei, sodass die Sitzverteilung der Parteien dem Anteil ihrer Wahlstimmen entspricht.
Die Fünfprozenthürde verhindert die Wahl einer Vielzahl kleinerer Parteien in den Bundestag: Parteien, die weniger als 5% aller Stimmen bekommen, dürfen nicht ins Parlament einziehen, es sei denn, mindestens drei ihrer Kandidat/innen wurden im Wahlkreis direkt gewählt.

 *Fotos:* Shutterstock (UK: VectorShop; USA: Globe Turner; D: Route 66)

## 1 Energy generation

windmill

coal mining

oil drilling

hydroelectric plant

geothermal energy

nuclear reactor

solar power

wind farm

**Thanks to the invention of** the solar cell, we can now **make use of** the sun's power as a source of green energy. We are not as dependent on fossil fuels, which cause pollution.

## 2 Transport

wheel

locomotive

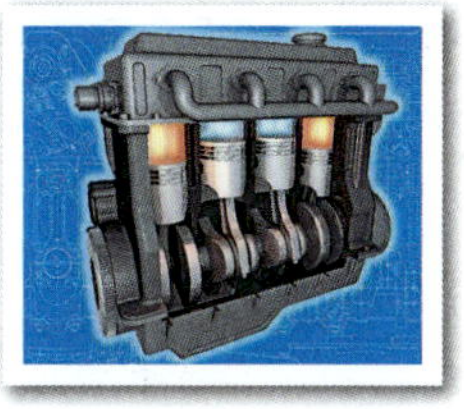
combustion engine

mass-produced cars

commercial flights

space shuttle

sat(ellite) nav(igation)

electric car

**The invention of** the locomotive and later the internal combustion engine **made it possible** for people to travel faster and for longer distances than riding or walking. **One of the positive effects of this** was that the world became smaller and mass travel **became possible**.

## 3 Household

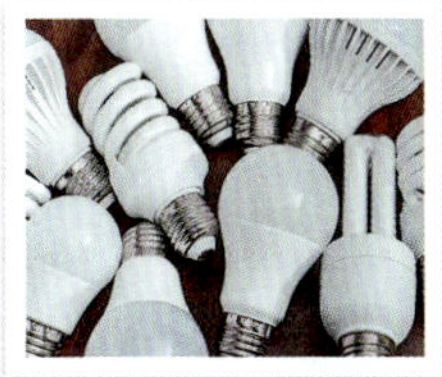
electric light

washing machine

radio

fridge

TV

microwave oven

home computer

smart home

**The impact of** the washing machine **cannot be overstated**. **It allowed** millions of women to enter the world of work as they no longer needed to spend most of the week washing the family's clothes. **One of the negative effects was** that millions of maids lost their jobs.

combustion [kəm'bʌstʃən] *Verbrennung* commercial flight [kə'mɜːʃl] *Passagier-, Linienflug* (to) drill *bohren* fossil fuel ['fɒsl ˌfjuːəl] *fossiler Brennstoff* geothermal energy [ˌdʒiːəʊ'θɜːml] *Erdwärme* hydroelectric plant [ˌhaɪdrəʊɪ'lektrɪk] *Wasserkraftwerk* invention [ɪn'venʃn] *Erfindung* locomotive [ˌləʊkə'məʊtɪv] maid [meɪd] *Dienstmädchen* (to) overstate [ˌəʊvə'steɪt] *überbewerten* space shuttle ['ʃʌtl] *Raumfähre* solar ['səʊlə]

*Fotos:* Shutterstock (Reihe 1, Bild 1: Fredy Thuerig, 2: Rasta777, 3: QiuJu Song, 4: ZoranOrcik, 5: N.Minton; R. 2, 1: nixki, 2: Wang An Qi, 3: WDG Photo; R. 3, 1: Lightspring, 2: jgorzynik, 3: Nikonaft, 4: Evgeniya Chertova, 5: BlueRingMedia; R. 4, 1: Dsculptor, 2: jennyt, 3: Nerthuz; R. 5, 1: anmbph, 2: Pro3DArtt, 3: Africa Studio, 4: Iconic Bestiary, 5: Dja65; R. 6, 1: MrGarry, 2: horiyan, 3: Brian A Jackson)

## 4 Telecommunications

telegraph

telephone

satellite

www

email

mobile phone

SMS

smartphone

**The main benefit** of mobile phones is that they have **made it possible** for people to stay in touch and find and send information wherever they are in the world. This **has had a huge influence on** how people communicate.

## 5 Agriculture

pasteurization

tractor

industrial greenhouse

combine harvester

pesticides

frozen foods

GM foods

agricultural drone

**The invention of** fertilizer and pesticides **enabled** farmers to increase the productivity of their land dramatically and to support the growing population of their country.

combine harvester [ˌkɒmbaɪn 'hɑːvɪstə] *Mähdrescher* fertilizer ['fɜːtəlaɪzə] *Düngemittel* GM (genetically modified) *gentechnisch verändert* influence *Einfluss* pasteurization [ˌpɑːstʃəraɪ'zeɪʃn] *Pasteurisierung* pesticide ['pestɪsaɪd] satellite ['sætəlaɪt]



*Fotos:* Shutterstock (Reihe 1, Bild 1: rook76, 2: Frannyanne, 3: Phonlamai Photo, 4: atm2003; R. 2, 1: Titov Nikolai, 2: Vangert, 3: Fine Art, 4: Es sarawuth; R. 3, 1: Mega Pixel, 2: ShendArt, 3: gtfour, 4: Orientaly; R. 4, 1: Adriano Kirihara, 2: defotoberg, 3: Alex_Traksel, 4: Suwin)

## Causes

- Burning **fossil fuels** in power stations
- **Carbon dioxide emissions** from transport
- **Deforestation**, legal and illegal
- Use of electricity and **resources** in industry and **manufacturing**
- Use of **chemical fertilizers** in farming
- **Methane** from cows and rice fields
- **Drilling** for **oil** and other natural resources
- Unnecessary **consumption**: shopping and using resources
- Waste: rubbish that is **dumped** after human use

## Consequences

- Melting polar ice cap
- Rising sea levels
- Rising sea temperatures
- **Extreme** weather: prolonged **heatwaves**, droughts, wildfires, and floods
- Crop **failure** and food **shortages**
- Death of coral reefs
- Health problems
- Increasing **income inequality** as the poor cannot **afford** higher prices for products and resources
- Conflict and wars between countries over resources
- Loss of animal habitat leading to **extinction**

## What governments can do

- Promote the use of alternative, greener and **sustainable** sources of energy: wind and **solar** power, **tidal** energy
- Increase **investment** in greener transport systems, **decommission power stations**
- International **cooperation** to fight pollution, overuse of resources and to protect wildlife
- Develop strategies to reduce human and industrial waste, and to increase recycling
- Introduce heavy fines for industrial pollution and waste
- Reduce or ban the use of chemical fertilizers and pesticides

## What individuals can do

- Form pressure groups to demand changes in the law
- Participate in peaceful protests, take part in marches and join campaigns to put pressure on governments and increase **awareness** of the issue
- Reduce your **carbon footprint**: buy less, recycle more, avoid products with unnecessary **packaging**, and share transport, or ride a bike to school or work
- Choose energy-**efficient lighting** and eat less meat

**Make a list of three things you already do to reduce your carbon footprint, and add two more you could do:**

__________ __________ __________

__________ __________

**(to) afford sth.** [ə'fɔːd] *sich etwas leisten* **awareness** [ə'weənəs] *Bewusstsein* **carbon dioxide** [ˌkɑːbən daɪ'ɒksaɪd] *Kohlendioxid* **carbon footprint** *$CO_2$-Fußabdruck* **chemical fertilizer** ['fɜːtəlaɪzə] *chemisches Düngemittel* **consequence** ['kɒnsɪkwəns] *Folge* **consumption** [kən'sʌmpʃn] *Verbrauch* **cooperation** [kəʊˌɒpə'reɪʃn] *Zusammenarbeit* **(to) decommission** [ˌdiːkə'mɪʃn] *stilllegen* **deforestation** [ˌdiːˌfɒrɪ'steɪʃn] *Abholzung* **(to) drill** *bohren* **(to) dump** *abladen* **efficient** [ɪ'fɪʃnt] *effizient* **emission** [i'mɪʃn] *Ausstoß* **extinction** [ɪk'stɪŋkʃn] *Aussterben* **extreme** [ɪk'striːm] *extrem* **failure** ['feɪljə] *Ausfall* **fossil fuel** ['fɒsl fjuːəl] *fossiler Brennstoff* **heatwave** ['hiːtweɪv] *Hitzewelle* **income** ['ɪnkʌm] *Einkommen* **inequality** [ˌɪnɪ'kwɒləti] *Ungleichheit* **investment** [ɪn'vestmənt] *Investition* **lighting** *Beleuchtung* **manufacturing** [ˌmænju'fæktʃərɪŋ] *Fertigung* **methane** ['miːθeɪn] *Methan* **oil** [ɔɪl] *Öl* **packaging** ['pækɪdʒɪŋ] *Verpackung* **power station** ['steɪʃn] *Kraftwerk* **prolonged** [prə'lɒŋd] *anhaltend* **resources** *(pl)* [rɪ'sɔːsɪz] *Ressourcen* **shortage** ['ʃɔːtɪdʒ] *Knappheit* **solar** ['səʊlə] *Sonnen-* **sustainable** [sə'steɪnəbl] *erneuerbar, nachhaltig* **tidal** ['taɪdl] *Gezeiten-*

*Foto:* Shutterstock/Photomontage

## Talking about genres

- I really like nature documentaries.
- There was a really good documentary on TV last night.
- It was **fascinating**.

- I just love thrillers.
- *Vertigo* is a **classic**.
- It's really gripping.

- Comedies are my favourite.
- There's a really good one on tonight.
- It's hilarious. It really made me laugh.

- I quite enjoy adventure films.
- The latest *Indiana Jones* is good fun.
- It's really exciting and very **imaginative**.

- I really enjoy **sci-fi** movies.
- I could watch them all day.
- I find them **thought-provoking**.

- I **can't stand** horror films.
- I couldn't sleep after watching *Dracula*.
- It's really scary.

- I saw a brilliant superhero film last night.
- I've seen *Spiderman* at least ten times.
- It's really **action-packed**.

- I'm not really into war films.
- I don't enjoy them at all.
- They're too **violent**.

- You can't beat a good musical.
- They're great fun.
- They're so enjoyable.

- I'm really into **romcoms**.
- They're great entertainment.
- They can be really **heart-warming** too.

### Talking about films

- The film's about …
- The plot was really interesting / a bit **unbelievable**.
- The film is set in London in the 1960s.

### Talking about the actors and characters

- The main characters are …
- Brad Pitt plays a …
- The film **stars** Eva Green as a … / in the role of a …
- I thought the acting was terrible.

### Talking about the people behind the film

- The film's director …
- It **is based on** real events / a real story / a novel by…
- The **screenplay** was by …

### Talking about elements of a film

- The soundtrack was great.
- The ending was very good / a real surprise / very **predictable**.
- The best scene was when …

**Write four positive things about a film that will help persuade a friend to go see it with you.**

____________________ ____________________

____________________ ____________________

**action-packed** *voller Action* **(to) be based on sth.** [beɪst] *auf etwas beruhen* **classic** ['klæsɪk] *Klassiker* **fascinating** ['fæsɪneɪtɪŋ] *faszinierend* **heart-warming** *herzerwärmend* **imaginative** [ɪ'mædʒɪnətɪv] *fantasievoll* **predictable** [prɪ'dɪktəbl] *voraussehbar* **romcom** ['rɒmkɒm] *romantische Komödie* **sci-fi** *(infml: science fiction)* ['saɪ faɪ] **screenplay** ['skriːnpleɪ] *Drehbuch* **(to) stand** *ausstehen* **(to) star** [stɑː] *in der Hauptrolle zeigen* **thought-provoking** [prə'vəʊkɪŋ] *zum Nachdenken anregend* **unbelievable** [ˌʌnbɪ'liːvəbl] *unglaublich* **violent** ['vaɪələnt] *gewalttätig*

 *Illustrationen:* Christian Bartz, Berlin

b) Match the highlighted parts of the extract to what they tell us about the protagonist, Marcus.

1 Marcus has childish things in his bedroom. 2 ______

2 He is feeling nervous and threatened. ______

3 To other people, he looks strange and has weird habits. ______

4 Marcus is a sensitive, observant and intelligent child. ______

5 He has a black sense of humour/imagination. ______

c) Consider the four parts that you did not use in a). Complete the sentence about Marcus's situation.

In parts 4, ___ , ___ and ___ , we learn that Marcus ______

d) Read the excerpt again. This time pay close attention to the atmosphere and tone conveyed. Ask yourself how the excerpt makes you feel and think about what it is about the text that gives you this/these feeling(s). Make notes.

Discuss with a partner. Compare your notes.

e) Now complete the table below about different aspects of the text.

| | **Descriptions/Examples/Line numbers** | **Atmosphere and tone created and their effects on the reader** |
|---|---|---|
| **Narrative technique** | The author uses a limited third-person narrator who knows only the thoughts and feelings of the protagonist. | ______ |
| **Setting(s)**<br>– Marcus's Bedroom | ______ | Gloomy and a bit scary. We feel and share the boy's worries and fears. |
| – School building and classrooms | ______ | The reader focuses only on Marcus's experience and his thoughts and feelings. |
| **Language**<br>– Repetition | ______ | It creates a sense of drama and rising tension. |
| – Imagery | ______ | It helps readers visualize the scene. Readers can 'see' that Marcus's negative thoughts at night are uncomfortable, even painful. |
| | "They patrolled up and down … like sharks" (ll. 33–34) | ______ |

f) Using your work from b)–e) as a basis, analyse how Marcus's feelings change over the course of the extract. In your answer, consider how the story is told (narrative and characterization techniques) and the use of language (atmosphere and tone).

## 10 LISTENING COURSE Dealing with listening tasks ➜ SB (pp. 72–73) • SMC 26 (pp. 71)

**You are going to listen to a news report, followed by a radio talk show. You can listen twice to each recording.**

**a) Before doing tasks b) to e), identify first what kind of listening task each one is.**

**b) 22 Listen to a news report. Complete the statements below by filling in the missing word(s).**

1 In ______________, a lot of students wrote to the Minister of Education to ask her to ______________________________.

2 They wrote the letters to support ______________ made by the ______________ on the topic on television.

3 The Ministry has ____________ to do what they asked because ____________ sets its own rules on the issue.

4 Research in the US shows that students there get an average of ____________________ per week and 75 % say it ____________________.

**c) 23 Now listen to the first part of a radio talk show. Circle the correct answer: A, B or C.**

1 Geoffrey believes that artificial intelligence …
- **A** will replace teachers in classrooms.
- **B** will mean the end of homework.
- **C** won't change things in schools at all.

2 Orla believes that homework helps …
- **A** parents to engage with their child's education.
- **B** students to repeat what they learnt in school.
- **C** students to develop positive life skills.

3 Orla says that …
- **A** we have to trust students.
- **B** students will always copy from the internet.
- **C** students need help in the long term.

4 Geoffrey says that in 2015, Finland …
- **A** started teaching creative writing in schools.
- **B** updated the way they teach English.
- **C** decided to teach keyboard skills instead of handwriting.

**d) 24 Listen to the next part of the talk show. Complete the table below by matching the opinions about homework A–F with the correct speaker. There is one more opinion than you need.**

**A** Accepts homework and rejects using AI.

**B** Enjoys it a lot and would never use AI.

**C** Wishes homework was done online with an AI teacher.

**D** Wishes homework was project-based and feels AI can help.

**E** Thinks homework is useless and would use AI if they could.

**F** Feels homework is helpful and cannot use AI.

| **Speaker** | **1 Alice** | **2 Calvin** | **3 Raj** | **4 Julie** | **5 Deepali** |
|---|---|---|---|---|---|
| **Opinion** | | | | | |

**e) 25 Listen to the final part of the talk show and complete the sentences in your exercise book.**

1 Orla points out that research on homework in Britain showed that …

2 Geoffrey believes that the survey shows the majority of students …

3 Geoffrey adds that if he were in charge of the education system, …

## 11 STUDY SKILLS Preparing for a panel discussion ➜ SB (p. 74) • SMC 23 (pp. 70)

a) Match the statements on the right below with the tips taken from p. 74 of your student's book. Draw lines.

1 When presenting your position, refer to views already expressed.

2 Show respect when referring to the views of others, even if you disagree with them.

3 Present your position in a structured way.

4 Make sure that everyone stays on topic.

5 Make sure that everyone has an equal chance to speak.

6 If you prefer not to be interrupted with a question, say so firmly, but politely.

**A** There are two points I'd like to make. First, there's … Second, I think it's also important that …

**B** I would be interested to hear your thoughts on that.

**C** Just let me finish this point, please, and then I'll answer your question.

**D** I see what you mean, but I'm afraid I don't share your view.

**E** As Melanie already said, this is one of the most important challenges young people face today …

**F** That's interesting but I think that's moving away from the topic we're discussing right now.

b) In any discussion, agreeing and disagreeing politely is very important. It is also important that everyone understands each other. Label each of the phrases below according to what they express (dis-/agreement) or request (explanation), as in the example.
A = agreement, D = disagreement, E = explanation

1 *You've got a good point there, I hadn't thought of that.* [A]

2 *I'm afraid I can't agree with you there because …* [ ]

3 *I agree 100 % and I would add …* [ ]

4 *Can you say a little more about that point?* [ ]

5 *I see what you're saying, but have you thought about …?* [ ]

6 *That's an excellent point.* [ ]

7 *I'm not sure you're right about that …* [ ]

8 *When you say […], what do you mean exactly?* [ ]

9 *I don't follow you. Could you say that again?* [ ]

10 *That's exactly how I see it and I would also say …* [ ]

c) You are going to play a discussion game with a partner. Before you do that, write phrases from this page and from SMC 22 (p. 70) on small cards. Make sure you have a good range of phrases to use e.g. to state your opinion, agree, disagree and ask for explanations. Choose a topic from the box or decide on your own topic. As you discuss the topic, use the phrases and put the cards in a pile. Whoever uses all of their cards first wins! When you are finished, play the game again with a different topic.

AI is dangerous · Social media should be banned for under 16s ·
Cyberbullying is not as bad as it used to be · 16-year-olds should be able to vote · Technology makes us lazy ·
Homework should be banned · We should all become vegetarian to save the environment

## 1 PRONUNCIATION Word stress

26 Say these words from Unit 3 aloud and underline the stressed syllable.
You can record your voice. Listen and check.

| | | | | | |
|---|---|---|---|---|---|
| 1 alternative | 3 complex | 5 digital | 7 exclusive | 9 (to) export | 11 radioactive |
| 2 battery | 4 controversial | 6 electricity | 8 (an) export | 10 parasite | 12 vision |

## 2 WORDS Defining words

a) Here are definitions of four new verbs which appear in this unit. Identify the verbs.

1 to stop someone doing something by law *to ban*

2 to pause for a short time ______

3 to connect a mobile phone to the electricity supply ______

4 to take one thing out and put another one in ______

b) Here are four more new verbs from the unit. Write your own definition for each one.

1 to depend on *to rely on*

2 to deliver ______

3 to recover ______

4 to predict ______

## 3 Using adverbs

Rewrite the following sentences, turning the underlined words or phrases into adverbs.
You might need to make changes to word order, etc.

1 The government has had to introduce an immediate ban on this.

*The government has had to ban this immediately.*

2 New species mean that we can make more economic use of resources.

______

3 Luckily the patient made a complete recovery.

______

4 We only have a vague understanding of the threat this issue might cause.

______

5 Could you please give a concise explanation of what the issue is?

______

6 It is my sincere hope we can come to an agreement on this matter.

______

## 4 Presenting your opinion in a panel discussion

**a) Match up the following phrases which appear frequently in panel discussions. There is more than one correct answer.**

1 I agree
2 You can't
3 I think
4 In my opinion,
5 I don't think
6 As we have seen,

| | |
|---|---|
| | we've got any new ideas. |
| | this is the best idea to proceed[1] with. |
| *1* | with what you're saying. |
| | just say that without giving an explanation. |
| | the problem isn't just going to go away. |
| | this needs to be done immediately. |

**b) Find out a little about the *Great Pacific Garbage Patch*[2] by doing an internet search. Comment on the following statements using sentence beginnings like in a).Write in your exercise book.**

1 We don't need to care about a bit of rubbish in the water.

*I disagree, because fish eat the plastic and we eat the fish.*

2 Plastic isn't dangerous so there's no problem.
3 The sea is so huge it can take all that rubbish.
4 Countries throw radioactive waste in the sea, so what does a bit of rubbish matter?
5 Well, can't we just clean it up?
6 It won't affect me or my children, so I don't care.

**c) You are a member of the local Association of Conservation[3] Volunteers, and you believe water pollution is becoming a huge problem. Prepare a two-minute introduction speech for a panel discussion stating your opinion and backing it up with facts.**

## Check: Speaking

a) Vergleiche deine Antworten mit den Lösungen auf Seite 88 im Workbook.
b) Schätze deine Antworten mit einem grünen oder roten Gesicht ein.

| | 🙂 | ☹ | |
|---|---|---|---|
| **1 PRONUNCIATION Word stress**<br>Konntest du die Wörter richtig und ohne Probleme aussprechen? | ○ | ○ | → 1 |
| **2 WORDS Defining words**<br>Konntest du die richtigen Wörter finden und umschreiben? | ○ | ○ | → 2 |
| **3 USING ADVERBS**<br>Konntest du die unterstrichenen Wendungen in adverbiale Konstruktionen umwandeln? | ○ | ○ | → 3, 4 |
| **4 Presenting your opinion in a panel discussion**<br>Konntest du vollständige Sätze bilden? Hast du verschiedene Redewendungen benutzt? Konntest du die Rede überzeugend präsentieren? | ○ | ○ | → 5 |

c) Wenn du dich rot eingeschätzt hast, schau dir die rechte Spalte an. Die Nummern führen dich zu den passenden Übungen im Skills Training (S. 54–55). Dort kannst du gezielt Speaking trainieren.

[1]proceed [prəˈsiːd] *fortfahren* [2]patch [pætʃ] *Fleck* [3]conservation [ˌkɒnsəˈveɪʃn] *Naturschutz*

## 1 PRONUNCIATION Word stress

27 Say the words and mark the stressed syllables. Then listen, check and say the words again.

1 analogy 2 application 3 compensate 4 electric 5 moderator 6 pilot

## 2 WORDS Improving your vocabulary

Identify the following words from the unit.

1 The process of improving something is known as ____________________.

2 Companies or people that have no money left are said to be ____________________.

3 Cancer treatments can leave your ____________________ system weak.

4 ____________________ products are grown without the use of artificial chemicals.

5 A ____________________ description is one which gives a lot of information in just a few words.

6 Topics which divide people are known as ____________________ issues.

7 ____________________ is the use of robots to do a job.

8 If you are not happy with a service you receive, it is your right to ____________________.

## 3 Speaking more naturally

a) Copy the table in your exercise book. Identify the following types of adverbs/adverbial phrases and write them in the right column.

after all · always · at first · calmly · carefully · constantly · even · for a few more years · in the garden · in the same place · later · of course · really · recently · regularly · right away · simply · still

| Sentence adverbs | Adverbs of frequency | Adverbs of indefinite time | Adverbs of manner | Adverbs of place | Adverbs of time | Adverbs of degree |
|---|---|---|---|---|---|---|
| | | | | | | |

b) Rewrite the following phrases using the adverbs/adverbial phrases in brackets ( ). Use your exercise book.

**TIP:** Remember the **sequence** for adverbials in most cases:
- **Front position:** *sentence adverbs*
- **Mid-position:** *adverbs of frequency* and *indefinite time*
- **End position:** *adverbs of manner, place* and *time*
- **Before the word they refer to:** *adverbs of degree*

1 We meet up to practise (in the same place/regularly).

*We meet up regularly to practise in the same place.*

2 We have to make sure we close the windows (always/carefully).

3 Our neighbours are complaining they can hear our music (constantly/in the garden).

4 We used to ignore them, but it has got worse (at first/recently).

5 They've started threatening to call the police if we don't stop (even/right away).

6 I told Mum I thought they were being rude, but she suggested we try talking to them (calmly/simply).

7 It's not going to be easy, but I'm going to do my best not to get annoyed when we go round to their house (later/of course/really).

## 4 Becoming more environmentally friendly

In your exercise book, rewrite the sentences using adjectives/adverbial phrases instead of the underlined adverbs. Make any necessary changes. One example has already been done for you.

1 We should deal with environment issues logically.

*We should deal with environment issues in a logical manner.*

2 It would be much easier to save the planet if we behaved more consciously.

3 Worryingly, some people – including politicians – still believe that global warming isn't real.

4 But, recently, more and more people have started living in a more 'environmentally friendly' way.

5 They believe, for instance, that paying a little more for renewable electricity helps the environment effectively.

6 We need to tell people explicitly what they need to do to save the planet from further damage.

## 5 PANEL DISCUSSION Organizing what you say ➜ *SMC 21–23 (pp. 69–70)*

Complete the table below with phrases you might hear during a panel discussion. Add your own phrases.

Although the lady makes a very good point … · As the lady mentioned … · *In my opinion …* · I think so too. · It often isn't as simple as that. · It's a known fact that … · Just a moment, please, to finish my point … · Personally, I believe … · So, to begin … · To open, I'd like to say … · We've already heard how … · You've already had your say.

| Good ways to start | Presenting my position | Agreeing and disagreeing | Referring to what someone said | Reacting to what someone is saying | Reacting to interruptions |
|---|---|---|---|---|---|
| | *In my opinion…* | | | | |
| | | | | | |
| | | | | | |
| | | | | | |
| | | | | | |
| | | | | | |
| | | | | | |
| | | | | | |
| | | | | | |
| | | | | | |
| | | | | | |
| | | | | | |

### Part one: Understanding a text

a) Match the typical instructions with the best description. There is one description you do not need. Draw lines.

| | |
|---|---|
| 1 Describe | A Present the main points or ideas |
| 2 Summarize | B Find and explain certain aspects |
| 3 Point out | C Show how the author structures the plot |
| | D Say in detail what someone or something is like |

b) Read the example exam task below. Then read the excerpt from the novel *About a Boy* on p. 48.
Tick (✓) the sentences which belong in a good answer to the exam task.
The sentences are not in the right order.

*Describe the situation Marcus finds himself in and how he deals with it.*

Marcus decides to go to school very early to avoid the kids who had bullied him the day before. ☐

The author uses similes to help readers understand better what the situation is like for Marcus: "he thought like boomerangs fly" (l. 10), "They patrolled … school corridors like sharks" (l. 34). ☐

The excerpt from the novel "About a Boy", written by Nick Hornby, deals with Marcus, a boy who has just started at a new school. ☐

It seems that the bullies noticed Marcus because he is new and because of how he looks and acts: Marcus has a bad haircut and on his first day at school he sang out loud in class. ☐

I think Marcus's situation is not that unusual because bullying happens quite often. ☐

The excerpt begins with Marcus alone in his bedroom and unable to sleep because he is worried about going to the new school. ☐

However, the situation turns bad for him in the English lesson. ☐

Marcus has a dark sense of humour which makes the reader like him more and feel sorry for him in his situation: "The kids who had given him a hard time yesterday were … off somewhere smoking and taking drugs …" (ll. 20–24). ☐

Marcus goes to his classroom, sits at his desk and at first, he feels safe. ☐

c) Now write your own answer to the task in about 80 words.
You may use the suitable sentences from b) but you should structure your answer correctly and add more details. Write in your exercise book.

### Part two: Analysing a text

a) Match the typical instruction with the best description.
There is one description you do not need. Draw lines.

| | |
|---|---|
| | A Describe and interpret aspects of a text in detail, possibly including a character's actions and the techniques used by the author. |
| 1 Explain | B Give reasons for events and/or actions in a text and point to relevant details. |
| 2 Analyse | C Give arguments or reasons for and against an issue raised by a text and come to a conclusion. |
| 3 Compare | D Show the similarities and differences between characters and/or situations portrayed in a text. |

b) You are going to analyse the extract from *The Whale Rider* by Witi Ihimaera on p. 59. First, look at the task below.

*Analyse how the author creates an atmosphere of drama and suspense. In doing so, look at the way the story is told (narrative technique, use of language).*

c) Now read parts of a sample answer to the task. Fill in the gaps with suitable words from the box.

build · climax · experience · first person · imagery · metaphors · narrator · paragraphs · scene · sense · structures · suspense

**1**

The author writes from the point of view of a ____________ unnamed narrator who is one of the men in the meeting house. This allows the reader to ____________ the story through his eyes and ears and to feel the "anticipation" (l. 7).

**2**

The character of Koro Apirana asks his audience many questions: "Is the tattoo there by accident or by design?" (ll. 48–49), "Why did a whale …?" (l. 49). These questions make the reader think about the answers too and create a ____________ of mystery, especially the final questions at the end of the extract: "Shall we live? Or shall we die?" These dramatic questions raise ____________ and make the reader want to read on.

**3**

The author uses a lot of ____________. The setting is described as a "stomach" (l. 6), which is unusual and makes the reader think what could happen to the people inside. Other images of nature in ____________, such as "The wind whistled through his words" (l. 61) and "His voice drifted through the air and hovered, waiting…"(ll. 68–69) help the reader imagine a stormy sea and powerful wind which ____________ the drama.

**4**

The author ____________ the text in a way that increases the tension slowly at first with short ____________ and pauses: "His voice fell silent"(ll. 15–16), "took a few thoughtful steps" (l. 28). It then goes more quickly as Koro Apirana tells the story of 'man' (ll. 30–41) and then uses pauses again (l. 43), before the dramatic ____________ at the end when the tribe cheers: "Our answer was an acclamation of pride …"(l. 71).

**5**

The ____________ describes the meeting house as a warm 'stomach' (l. 6) while outside there is the sea: "Suddenly he gestured to the sea" (ll. 45–46), and the wind: "The wind whistled" (l. 61). This makes the meeting house the centre of the dramatic ____________ with a threatening storm blowing outside.

## Part three: Creative writing tasks

### The structure of a creative writing task

**a) Look at the example writing task below and read parts 1–6 of a sample answer. What is the correct order?**

*What do you think about* Click'd*? Comment on Allie's product. Include the following aspects: risks and advantages of Allie's product / the role social media play in your life / your opinion on personally using* Click'd.

**1** In conclusion, I think Allie has a great idea for an app, but I don't think I personally would use it. I have enough social media apps and I am happy with the friends that I have.

**2** However, if I used the app to find friends, I would only have friends who are like me and that would be boring. That is a danger of an app like Click'd.

**3** In my opinion, Click'd is a great app with many benefits. Firstly, it helps you connect with people who share your interests very fast and easily. I believe this would be useful if you were not very outgoing or moved to a new school or town where you didn't know anyone.

**4** But I deleted a lot of the apps and now I try to have a balance. As part of that, Sunday is my screen-free day and actually the most relaxing day of my week.

**5** Secondly, the app is very user-friendly – all you need is a smartphone and some answers to a few questions. In my view, the most interesting and fun thing about the app would be to find out who I match most with.

**6** If *Click'd* were real, it wouldn't be much different from other types of social media and I know them all very well. Too well, in fact. I used to spend too much time on social media and I didn't have any hobbies.

→ Correct order: ☐, ☐, ☐, ☐, ☐, ☐

**b) Now match parts 1–6 to the aspects of the writing task. Write in the numbers.**

1 risks and advantages of Allie's product — Parts: ______

2 the role social media plays in your life — Parts: ______

3 your opinion on personally using *Click'd* — Parts: ______

### The style of a creative writing task

**a) Look at the sample task below. Answer the questions which follow. Write in your exercise book.**

*Your school is holding a special day to help young people deal with bullying. Write an article for your school website. Include the following aspects: anyone can suffer bullying / bullying doesn't just happen in the school yard / examples of positive ways of dealing with bullying.*

**1** What form should my text take? **2** Who is the audience for my text? **3** What specific points should I address?

**b) Look at another sample task. It is based on the excerpt from the novel *About a Boy* on p. 48.**

*Marcus walks home from school. On his way, he sees some school bullies. Write the continuation of the story. Include: how Marcus deals with the bullies / what Marcus tells his mother when he gets home / how his mother reacts / a decision they make together.*

> **TIP:** When you write the continuation of a story, it is important to use the same narrative technique and writing style as the original text.

**Take a close look at the style of the novel excerpt and tick (✓) the correct boxes.**

| | | |
|---|---|---|
| The story is told by … | **A** ☐ a first-person narrator. | **B** ☐ a third-person narrator. |
| It is written in the … | **A** ☐ simple present. | **B** ☐ simple past. |
| It includes … | **A** ☐ narration and a little dialogue. | **B** ☐ narration and a lot of dialogue. |
| The narrator has … | **A** ☐ a matter-of-fact, serious tone. | **B** ☐ a sarcastic, ironic tone sometimes. |

### Practice task

**Read the extract from *The Whale Rider* by Witi Ihimaera and do the tasks which follow as if you were under exam conditions. Allow yourself ten minutes at most to choose the task and forty-five minutes for writing.**

*A number of whales, including a bull (male) whale with a strange tattoo, have landed on the beach of a small New Zealand town. The whales are in danger of dying. The local Māori chief, Koro Apirana, gathers the men of the tribe in their meeting house.*

Inside the stomach of the meeting house there was warmth, bewilderment, strength and anticipation, waiting to be soldered into a unity by the words of our chief, Koro Apirana. […]
'Well, boys,' he said, 'there are not many of us. I count twenty-six —'
'Don't forget me, Koro,' a six-year-old interjected.
'Twenty-seven, then,' Koro Apirana smiled, 'so we all have to be one in body, mind, soul and spirit. But first we have to agree on what we must do.' His voice fell silent. 'To explain, I have to talk philosophy and I never went to no university. My university was the school of hard knocks —'
'That's the best school of all,' someone yelled.
'So I have to explain in my own way. Once, our world was one where the Gods talked to our ancestors and man talked with the Gods. Sometimes the Gods gave our ancestors special powers. For instance, our ancestor Paikea' — Koro Apirana gestured to the apex of the house — 'was given power to talk to whales and to command them. In this way, man, beasts and Gods lived in close communion with one another.'
Koro Apirana took a few thoughtful steps back and forward.
'But then,' he continued, 'man assumed a cloak of arrogance and set himself up above the Gods. He even tried to defeat Death, but failed. As he grew in his arrogance he started to drive a wedge through the original oneness of the world. In the passing of Time he divided the world into that half he could believe in and that half he could not believe in. The real and the unreal. The natural and supernatural. The present and the past. The scientific and the fantastic. He put a barrier between both worlds and everything on his side was called rational and everything on the other side was called irrational. Belief in our Maori Gods,' he emphasised, 'has often been considered irrational.'
Koro Apirana paused again. He had us in the palms of his hands and was considerate about our ignorance, but I was wondering what he was driving at. Suddenly he gestured to the sea.
'You have all seen the whale,' he said. 'You have all seen the sacred sign tattooed on its head. Is the tattoo there by accident or by design? Why did a whale of its appearance strand itself here and not at Wainui? Does it belong in the real world or the unreal world?'
'The real,' someone called.
'Is it natural or supernatural?'
'It is supernatural,' a second voice said.
Koro Apirana put up his hands to stop the debate. 'No,' he said, 'it is both. It is a reminder of the oneness which the world once had. It is the birth cord joining past and present, reality and fantasy. It is both. It is both,' he thundered, 'and if we have forgotten the communion then we have ceased to be Maori.'
The wind whistled through his words. 'The whale is a sign,' he began again. 'It has stranded itself here. If we are able to return it to the sea, then that will be proof that the oneness is still with us. If we are not able to return it, then this is because we have become weak. If it lives, we live. If it dies, we die. Not only its salvation but ours is waiting out there.'
Koro Apirana closed his eyes. His voice drifted in the air and hovered, waiting for a decision.
'Shall we live? Or shall we die?'
Our answer was an acclamation of pride in our tribe.
Koro Apirana opened his eyes. 'Okay then, boys. Let's go down there and get on with it.'

a) **Summarize** Koro Apirana's view of the how modern society has developed.

b) **Analyse** how Koro Apirana tries to convince his audience. Look at how he addresses his audience, uses questions, etc.

c) Here you can choose between two different options. Do only 1 or 2.

1 You read an article on a news website which says that young people today believe technology has all the answers to humanity's problems. Write a comment on the website. Include the following aspects: your opinion on whether people rely too much on technology / whether you personally think that technology has all the answers to humanity's problems.

2 You were in the audience for Koro Apirana's speech and left with the others afterwards. Write a diary entry for that evening. Include the effect of Koro Apirana's speech on you and the group / what you and the others did immediately after the speech / whether your actions were successful.

## 1 Skimming and scanning ➜ SB (p. 163)

SKIMMING

**Step 1:** Sieh dir die folgenden Textteile an, um zu sehen, worum es im Text geht:
- Überschrift und Unterüberschriften
- Bilder und Bildunterschriften
- den ersten Satz jedes Absatzes – dieser Satz ist meist der *topic sentence*, der die Hauptidee des Absatzes nennt
- den letzten Absatz, der oft eine Zusammenfassung des Textes enthält.

**Step 2:** Fasse für dich selbst den Text in ein paar Worten zusammen. Wenn dir das ohne Probleme gelingt, dann weißt du, um was es in dem Text geht – und dass dein Skimming erfolgreich war.

**TIPP:** Mache dir um unbekannten Wortschatz erst mal keine Gedanken – dafür ist Zeit, wenn du feststellst, dass der Text für dich geeignet ist.

SCANNING

**Step 1:** Überlege dir *keywords*, die für dein Thema oder deine Frage relevant sind. Suchst du z. B. nach den Öffnungszeiten eines Museums, dann könnten das Wörter sein wie *open, hours* oder *days*.

**Step 2:** Überfliege den Text und suche nach den *keywords*. Du kannst dabei mit dem Finger in einer „S-Form" durch den Text gehen.

**Step 3:** Lies die Textstelle, die dein *keyword* enthält, um zu sehen, ob sie die gewünschten Informationen enthält. Wenn nicht, scanne weiter.

**TIPP:** Wenn du mit Texten im Internet arbeitest, kann dein Browser dir viel Arbeit abnehmen. Mit Strg+F (Cmd+F am Mac) kannst du nach deinen *keywords* suchen und nur die Textstellen lesen, in denen ein *keyword* markiert ist.

## 2 Marking up a text ➜ SB (p. 163)

**Step 1:** Lies die Aufgabe genau und überlege, welche Informationen du zur Beantwortung brauchst. Behalte dies beim Lesen des Textes im Kopf.

**Step 2:** Markiere nur wichtige Informationen (z. B. durch Unterstreichen oder mit einem Textmarker). Oft reicht es, ein oder zwei Wörter in einem Satz zu markieren.

**Step 3:** Mach dir Notizen am Rand, z. B. kurze Überschriften oder Stichwörter, die den Inhalt zusammenfassen. (➜ *SMC 41*)

**TIPP:**
1. Verwende unterschiedliche Farben für unterschiedliche Aufgaben/Fragestellungen.
2. Markiere wirklich nur Stichwörter, sonst wird es unübersichtlich.

## 3 Structuring texts ➜ SB (p. 164)

Ein guter Text besteht in der Regel aus den folgenden drei Teilen:

- **Einleitung *(introduction)*:**
  Hier steht, worum es in dem gesamten Text geht.
- **Hauptteil *(main body)*:**
  Dieser Teil ist in mehrere Absätze gegliedert und präsentiert die Details (Fakten, Beispiele etc.) zu deinem Thema.
- **Schluss *(conclusion)*:**
  Hier gibst du deinem Text ein passendes, interessantes Ende.

PARAGRAPHS

Längere Texte sind einfacher zu lesen, wenn sie in Absätze eingeteilt sind. Dabei solltest du folgende Dinge beachten:
- Fange für jeden neuen Aspekt einen neuen Absatz an.
- Beginne mit einem interessanten *topic sentence*.
- Beende deinen Text im letzten Absatz mit einer Zusammenfassung oder etwas Persönlichem.

TOPIC SENTENCES

Jeder Absatz sollte mit einem Einleitungssatz beginnen. Er beschreibt, worum es in dem Absatz geht. Wichtige Dinge, die du in einem *topic sentence* ansprechen kannst, sind z. B.
- **Orte:** *My trip to Berlin was exciting.*
- **Personen:** *The Beatles are the most famous band in the world.*
- **Aktivitäten:** *Lots of people ride their bike every day.*

My Trip to New Orleans

Last summer I wanted to go to New Orleans because I like big cities.

First I had to find some information on New Orleans. So I went online. I found a website with some interesting information on the sights and I also found a list of hostels for New Orleans.

I did not want to go to New Orleans alone, so I had to find someone to go with me. I called most of my friends and told them about my plan. Some of my friends did not want to spend their holidays in a big city and others had no money for the trip. But my friend Judith agreed to go with me. We decided to go in August.

Judith and I spent two lovely weeks in New Orleans. We went to the French Market and enjoyed the fantastic food there. We stayed in a lovely hostel and met lots of really nice people. Before we went home we spent a whole afternoon in the French Quarter.

This was one of the best summer holidays I ever had. Go to New Orleans – it's fantastic!

## 4 Writing good sentences ➔ SB (p. 165)

Gute Texte bestehen aus abwechslungsreichen Sätzen. Die folgenden Techniken helfen dir, den Stil deiner Texte zu verbessern.

### Adjektive

Beschreibe Dinge, Orte und Menschen näher mit Adjektiven:

- *a **bright** face*
- *a **fantastic** trip*

Stell aber sicher, dass du **good, bad** und **nice** nicht zu häufig verwendest. Ersetze sie durch genauere Adjektive:

- *a **nice** teacher: a **friendly** teacher, a **helpful** teacher, …*
- *a **good** book: an **interesting** book, a **funny** book, …*

### Adverbien

Verwende Adverbien, um Handlungen näher zu beschreiben, und Ausdrücke wie **really, very, a bit** etc., um Aussagen zu verdeutlichen oder zu verstärken:

- *They walked home **slowly**.*
- *She talked **quietly**.*
- *It was a **really** sad story.*
- *The houses are **very** high.*

### Konjunktionen

Konjunktionen wie **and, but** oder **because** geben deinen Sätzen eine klare, gut nachvollziehbare Struktur:

- *We went to the London Eye, **but** it was very expensive.*

### Relativsätze

Relativsätze verbinden Sätze oder geben mehr Informationen zu einer Sache oder einer Person:

- *This is the shop **which** sells the best ice cream in Berlin.*

### Zeitangaben

Adverbiale Bestimmungen der Zeit helfen Lesenden, sich in Texten zeitlich zurechtzufinden. Verwende *time markers*, um …

- die **Reihenfolge von Ereignissen** zu verdeutlichen: *at first, next, finally, …*
- zu zeigen, **wie viel Zeit** zwischen einzelnen Ereignissen vergeht: *for half an hour, just two minutes later, …*
- zu verdeutlichen, **wie langsam oder schnell** etwas passiert: *immediately, it took hours, faster than I could look, …*
- zu sagen, wenn etwas **zeitgleich** passiert: *while I was waiting, during the lesson, as we came round the corner, …*
- die **Ereignisse eines Textes/einer Geschichte** zeitlich einzuordnen: *two summers ago, last Halloween, on my way home from school yesterday, …*

## 5 Writing a formal letter or email ➔ SB (p. 166)

Wenn du einen Brief oder eine Mail an eine Organisation, einen potenziellen Arbeitgeber oder Ähnliches schreibst, sollte dein Schreiben gewissen formalen Regeln folgen.

Schreibe **deine Adresse** (ohne Namen) oben rechts. Verwende keine typisch deutschen Buchstaben wie ä, ö, ü oder ß.

Schreibe die volle Anschrift (mit Namen, wenn du ihn weißt) des **Adressaten** auf die linke Seite.

Schreibe das **Datum** auf die rechte Seite.

Sage kurz im **Betreff**, worum es geht.

**Beginne deinen Brief/deine Mail** mit *Dear Sir or Madam*, wenn du keinen genauen Ansprechpartner hast. Ansonsten schreibe *Dear Mr/Mrs/Ms …* (mit Komma danach, in den USA auch oft mit Doppelpunkt). Fange danach immer groß an.

Nenne den **Grund des Schreibens** im ersten Absatz.

- Ergänze weitere Informationen in den folgenden Absätzen.
- Verwende **Langformen** *(I am/We are/I would)* **statt Kurzformen** *(I'm/We're/I'd)* und Abkürzungen.

Wenn du den Adressaten um etwas bittest (z. B. Informationen), **bedanke dich** im Voraus.

**Beende das Schreiben** mit *Yours sincerely*, wenn du den Namen des Ansprechpartners kennst; ansonsten schreibe *Yours faithfully*.

Kruemelstrasse 12
12345 Berlin
Germany

John Keats
Donne House
Ipswich IP3 4BA
United Kingdom

3 March 2019

Enquiry about exchange programme

Dear Mr Keats,

I am writing to enquire about the exchange programme which I saw advertised in The English Magazine.

I have been studying English at school for six years now and I would like to take part in an exchange programme to improve my English.

Could you please tell me if you offer any exchange programmes for one month in the summer? It would be helpful to know about dates, application procedures and the cost of such an exchange. Any additional information would be very welcome.

Thank you for your help. I look forward to hearing from you soon.

Yours sincerely,

Paul Panther

Paul Panther

## 6 Making an outline ➔ *SB (p. 167)*

Jede Art von Text profitiert davon, wenn du dir vorab überlegst, was du in welcher Reihenfolge schreiben willst. Damit leistest du schon eine Menge Vorarbeit und erleichterst dir das Schreiben.

- Für eine Erörterung (➔ *SMC 7*) kannst du in deiner Outline die Argumente sortieren, die du im Text bringen möchtest.
- Bei einer Zusammenfassung (➔ *SMC 13*) kannst du hier die wichtigsten Punkte festhalten.

*Outline*
*1 Title*
*2 Introduction*
*Key words*
*3 Main body*
*Sub-heading*
*Key words*
*4 Conclusion*
*Key words*

## 7 Writing an argumentative essay ➔ *SB (p. 167)*

Wenn du eine Erörterung schreibst – also schriftlich für oder gegen etwas argumentierst –, solltest du deinen Text gut strukturieren und schlüssig präsentieren.

PLANUNGSPHASE

**Step 1:** Lies die Aufgabe sorgfältig durch.
**Step 2:** Sammle Ideen und mache erste Notizen. Schreibe alle Argumente pro und contra auf, die dir einfallen.
**Step 3:** Ordne deine Argumente, z. B. in Form einer Outline (➔ *SMC 6*). Hebe das wichtigste Argument hervor – damit solltest du deinen Hauptteil beenden, denn das merken sich die Lesenden am ehesten.

SCHREIBPHASE

**Step 1:** Schreibe deine Einleitung. Sage kurz, um welches Thema es geht, ohne deine eigene Meinung dazu zu äußern.
**Step 2:** Im Hauptteil präsentierst du dann die Argumente, die du dir überlegt hast.

*Outline/Notes*
*1 Introduction*
*Introduce the topic*
*2 Main body*
*1st paragraph: arguments con*
*– argument 1*
*– argument 2 etc.*
*2nd/3rd paragraph: arguments pro*
*– argument 1*
*– argument 2 etc.*
*End with strongest argument!*
*3 Conclusion*
*Sum up your arguments.*
*Give your opinion.*

## 8 Writing an opinion piece / a comment ➔ *SB (p. 168)*

Im Gegensatz zu einer Erörterung (➔ SMC 7), in der du beide Seiten eines Themas vorstellst und dann zu einer Schlußfolgerung kommst, geht es bei einem ***opinion piece*** (Kommentar oder Meinungsartikel) darum, deine persönliche Meinung zu präsentieren und mit Argumenten zu stützen.

PLANUNGSPHASE

**Step 1:** Sammle Ideen und mache erste Notizen. Was willst du sagen? Was willst du erreichen? Welche Fakten oder Zitate unterstützen deine Meinung? Hast du schon eine Lösungsidee, von der du andere überzeugen möchtest?
**Step 2:** Überlege dir eine gute Überschrift. Sie sollte die Aufmerksamkeit der Leser wecken und sie neugierig machen.
**Step 3:** Erstelle eine Outline. (➔ *SMC 6*) Überlege, wie du deine Argumentation/ Meinung unterstützen kannst (Fakten, Statistiken, Zitate etc.).
**Step 4:** Recherchiere passendes Material. (➔ *SMC 27*)

SCHREIBPHASE

**Step 1:** Beginne dein ***opinion piece*** mit einem kurzen Absatz zu dem Thema und deiner Meinung dazu.
**Step 2:** Präsentiere Argumente für deine Meinung in den folgenden Absätzen und ergänze sie mit weiteren Fakten, Beispielen oder Zitaten. Dabei kannst du viele der Redemittel verwenden, die du auch bei einer Erörterung nutzt. (➔ *SMC 7*)
**Step 3:** Im letzten Absatz, der ***conclusion***, wiederholst du noch einmal deine Meinung und schlägst entweder eine Lösung vor (wenn es sich z. B. um ein Problem handelt) oder forderst deine Leser auf, etwas zu tun.

Outline / Notes
1. Headline
- catch your readers' attention (clear statement, provocative question etc.)
2. First paragraph
- state your topic AND your opinion clearly (keep it short!)
- keep your readers interested
3. Supporting paragraphs
use statistics, facts, quotes etc. to back up your main statement
4. Final paragraph / Conclusion
- restate your opinion
- suggest a solution or call for action

## 9 Writing a letter/email to the editor ➜ SB (p. 169)

Ein Leserbrief (oder heutzutage meist eine Leser-Mail) ist eine Reaktion auf einen Artikel in einer Zeitung oder einem Magazin und ist im Aufbau eine Mischung aus einem formellen Brief und einem comment.

### VORBEREITUNG

- Lies den Artikel, auf den du reagieren willst, noch einmal gründlich durch. Mach dir dabei Notizen zu den Punkten, auf die du dich beziehen willst.
- Ordne deine Notizen in einer Gliederung (➜ *SMC 6*). Notiere dir auch gleich deine Argumente und Belegstellen/Beispiele dafür.

### FORMELLES

- Für einen Brief hältst du dich an dieselben Regeln wie bei einem formellen Brief (➜ *SMC 5*). Bedenke bei der Adresse, dass du das Schreiben an den Autor oder die Autorin des Artikels richtest sowie an die Adresse der Zeitung.
- Wenn du den Namen nicht kennst, schreibe an *The Editor*. Die Adresse für Leserbriefe findest du in der Regel im Impressum der Zeitung.
- Die Email-Adresse für Leserbriefe findest du oft auf der Webseite unter *Contact*.

### SCHREIBEN

- **Beginne deinen Brief/deine Mail** mit ***Dear Sir or Madam*** wenn du keinen genauen Ansprechparntner hast. Ansonsten schreibe ***Dear Mr/Mrs/Ms …*** (mit Komma danach, in den USA auch oft mit Doppelpunkt). Fange danach immer groß an.
- **Einleitung:** Im ersten Absatz nennst du den **Artikel und die Ausgabe, in der er erschien,** damit dein Leserbrief einfach zugeordnet werden kann. Du kannst hier auch schon sagen, wie du auf den Artikel reagieren wirst (*agreeing/disagreeing/ commenting/criticizing*):
  *I have read your article "Into the future", published in The Newspaper on 27 September 2022, which deals with … I am writing to you in order to … / I agree/disagree with you on …*
- Im **Hauptteil** gehst du auf einen oder mehrere Punkte des Artikels und deine Meinung dazu ein. Du bringst hier nur Argumente an, die deine Perspektive stützen.
- Nutze für jedes neue Argument einen neuen Absatz, aber halte dich relativ kurz. Ein Leserbrief ist kein Aufsatz, sondern ein Schreiben, in dem du kurz und klar deine Meinung zu einem Artikel gibst.
- Bleibe sachlich und möglichst neutral, auch wenn es um deine Meinung geht. Verwende formale Sprache und vermeide Kurzformen.
- **Schluss:** Beende deinen Brief oder deine E-Mail mit ***Yours sincerely***, wenn du den Namen des Ansprechpartners kennst; ansonsten schreibe ***Yours faithfully*** (wenn du an einen amerikanischen Kontakt schreibst, kannst du in diesem Fall auch *Yours truly* schreiben). Bei einem Brief tippe deinen Namen am Ende, aber lasse ausreichend Platz für deine **Unterschrift**.

**LANGUAGE HELP:**
Hier sind ein paar Redemittel, die du in deinem Leserbrief verwenden kannst:

Agreeing
- *First of all, I would like to approve/agree with you / …*
- *You are right in writing/saying/…*
- *You have a point in saying/mentioning/writing that …*

Disagreeing
- *I am afraid I do not quite agree …*
- *I am not convinced that …*
- *You have a point in saying …, but I would like to point out that …*
- *However/Nevertheless, it could also be said that …*

Commenting/Criticizing
- *I would like to add that …*
- *Moreover, I would like to point out that …*
- *It is true that …, but on the other hand it should be made clear that …*

## 10 Writing an article ➜ SB (p. 170)

Artikel sind Texte, die in der Regel zur Veröffentlichung in einer Zeitung, Zeitschrift oder einem Blog geschrieben werden. Es gibt verschiedene Arten von Artikeln wie z. B. Nachrichten, Berichte (➜ *SMC 11*), Kommentare (➜ *SMC 8*) oder Rezensionen (➜ *SMC 12*).

Für einen guten Artikel solltest du folgende Punkte beachten:

### PUBLIKUM

Für wen schreibst du? Wer ist die **Zielgruppe** deines Artikels? Wenn du z. B. einen Artikel über politische Demonstration in deiner Stadt schreibst, hast du möglicherweise andere Leser als bei einem Artikel über das letzte Spiel des lokalen Fußballvereins. Das Wissen über die Zielgruppe hilft dir, sie richtig anzusprechen und z. B. eine Überschrift zu wählen, die das Interesse dieser Leser weckt.

### AUFMERKSAMKEIT

Wie erregst du die Aufmerksamkeit möglicher Leser? Dein Artikel kann noch so gut sein – wenn ihn keiner liest, nützt das nichts. Eine gute **Überschrift** hilft, ebenso wie ein interessanter **Einstieg**. Beides kann z. B. provokant sein oder witzig – wichtig ist, dass es Leser dazu bringt, bei deinem Artikel "hängen zu bleiben".
Ein gutes Mittel sind z. B. rhetorische Fragen oder ein Zitat zum Thema (ähnlich wie bei Präsentationen, ➜ *SMC 30*).

**TIPP:** Aufmerksamkeit erregende Überschriften heißen im Internet ***"clickbait"***, also Klick-Köder. Wenn du das nächste Mal Artikel suchst, achte darauf, ***warum*** du bestimmte Artikel liest und andere nicht: Was an den Überschriften hat dich gereizt, weiterzulesen oder den Link anzuklicken?

### INTERESSE

Ein Artikel funktioniert nur, wenn deine Leser auch **bis zum Ende interessiert** bleiben und nicht nach ein oder zwei Absätzen aussteigen. Halte das Interesse hoch, indem du deinen Text z. B. mit Beispielen, Anekdoten und Zitaten anreicherst.

### ZITATE

Wenn du in deinem Artikel Zitate einbauen möchtest, denke daran, dass diese immer als solche erkennbar sein müssen:

- Setze wörtliche Zitate immer in Anführungszeichen („…“ im Deutschen, "…" im Englischen).
  Für ein Zitat innerhalb eines Zitats setzt du einfache Anführungszeichen (s. u.).
- Gib die **Quelle des Zitats** an, entweder in Klammern direkt nach dem Zitat oder in einer Fußnote auf der Seite. Das gilt auch für Zitate innerhalb von Zitaten:
  *Johnson says, "You have to name your sources even if it's a 'quote within a quote' (Smith, Using quotes, p. 25)." (Johnson, How to quote, p. 12)*
- Verändere den **Wortlaut des Zitats** nicht. Du kannst Wörter auslassen, musst dies aber durch drei Punkte **(…)** deutlich machen.

**TIPP:** Quellenangaben machst du so:
- **Bücher:** Autor, Titel, Seitenangabe, also z. B. *A. Meier, Buch ohne Titel, S. 15*
- **Webseiten:** URL und ggf. Titel, z. B. *www.wikipedia.de: William Shakespeare*

### LESBARKEIT

Erleichtere das Lesen des Artikels, indem du ihn mit Zwischenüberschriften in **Abschnitte** unterteilst und gut strukturierst. (➜ *SMC 3*) Wichtig ist eine gute Planung mithilfe einer **Outline**, mit der du den Artikel schon vorstrukturierst. (➜ *SMC 6*) Überlege, wie du in deiner Einleitung das Interesse der Leser wecken kannst, ohne schon vorwegzunehmen, was im Rest des Artikels kommt.

**TIPP:** Ein Artikel ist **kein Aufsatz**, bei dem du in der Einleitung die Fragestellung wiederholst und andeutest, wie du sie lösen willst. Bei einem Artikel geht es eher darum, in der Einleitung das Interesse der Leser zu wecken und sie zum Weiterlesen oder Nachdenken zu bewegen.

### ABSCHLUSS

Ein guter Artikel regt die Leser auch über die Zeit des Lesens hinaus noch zum Nachdenken an. Der letzte Absatz bestimmt entscheidend den Gesamteindruck mit – der Schluss ist das, was deinen Lesern in Erinnerung bleibt und sie im besten Fall weiter beschäftigt.

Dies kannst du erreichen, in dem du z. B. nochmal auf ein Zitat in deiner Einleitung zurückkommst oder hier ein weiteres anbringst. Wenn du im ersten Absetz eine rhetorische Frage gestellt hast, kannst du im letzten Absatz diese beantworten oder noch einmal stellen. Oder du stellst eine weiterführende Frage, die sich aus dem Informationen in deinem Artikel ergibt.

## 11 Writing a report ➔ *SB (p. 171)*

In einem Bericht stellst du übersichtlich und gut verständlich Fakten dar, z. B. zu einem Ereignis oder einem Vorfall.

### STRUKTUR

Wie jeder Text sollte ein Bericht aus einer **Überschrift**, einer **Einleitung**, einem **Hauptteil** und einem **Schluss** bestehen. (➔ *SMC 3*)
In einer Gliederung (➔ *SMC 6*) kannst du die Struktur schon anlegen und für jeden Textteil eine Überschrift notieren sowie Stichwörter dazu ergänzen. Wenn du viele Informationen im Hauptteil unterbringen willst, verwende auch Unterüberschriften.

### STICHWÖRTER

In der **Einleitung** sagst du kurz, was passiert ist. Dabei kannst du schon knapp die wichtigsten ***wh*-Fragen** beantworten, bevor du im Hauptteil näher darauf eingehst. In deiner Gliederung (➔ *SMC 6*) solltest du deswegen für die Einleitung deine Stichworte auf die Fragen **Who?, What?, When?, Where?** und **Why?** konzentrieren.
Im **Hauptteil** eines Berichtes stehen die **Details** des Ereignisses, meist in chronologischer Reihenfolge. Hier werden die ***wh***-Fragen genauer beantwortet, weswegen du in der Gliederung für den Hauptteil weitere Stichworte zu den einzelnen Fragen sammeln solltest.

Im **Schlussabsatz** bringst du deinen Bericht zum Abschluss, indem du z. B. kurz das Ergebnis oder die Folgen des beschriebenen Ereignisses darstellst.

**TIPP:** Ein Bericht soll objektiv sein und Fakten darstellen. Konzentriere dich bei deinen ***keywords*** in der Gliederung darauf, die 5 ***wh***-Fragen zu beantworten:
- **What** happened?
- **Who** did what?
- **When** did it happen?
- **Where** did it happen?
- **Why** did it happen?

Denk daran, dass ein Bericht im **simple past** geschrieben wird. Du solltest also deine Stichworte auch gleich so notieren.

## 12 Writing a review ➔ *SB (p. 171)*

In einer Rezension zu einem Buch oder einem Film gibst du dem Leser standardmäßig folgende Informationen: Autor/Regisseur, Darsteller, Charaktere, Handlung etc. Am Ende gibts du deine persönliche Meinung zum Film oder Buch ab.

### VORBEREITUNG

**Step 1:** Lies das Buch bzw. gucke den Film. Notiere dir, was dir besonders auffällt – positiv, negativ oder einfach als bemerkenswert.
**Step 2:** Ergänze deine Notizen mit Informationen über das Buch bzw. den Film. Am besten strukturierst du die Notizen gleich, z. B. in einer Tabelle. Folge dabei schon der Struktur der Rezension (siehe rechts).

### SCHREIBPHASE

**Step 1:** Schreibe einen ersten Entwurf.
- Verwende das **simple present**.
- Beginne mit der **Einleitung**, die die grundlegenden Informationen enthält.
- Im **Hauptteil** schreibe mithilfe deiner Notizen eine kurze Zusammenfassung des Inhalts (ohne zuviel zu verraten – besonders nicht das Ende) und gib mehr Informationen zu den Charakteren.
- Am **Schluss** gib deine Meinung zum Buch oder Film. Sage, weshalb du glaubst, dass man das Buch lesen/den Film sehen sollte (oder nicht). Eventuell erwähne, für welche Zielgruppe das Buch/der Film gedacht ist.
- Falls du es noch nicht getan hast, überlege dir eine **Überschrift**, die das Interesse der Leser weckt.

**Step 2:** Überarbeite deinen Text. (➔ *SMC 14, 15*)

| | |
|---|---|
| *Headline* | • *catch your readers' attention*<br>• *hint at your opinion or the book's/movie's content* |
| *Introduction* | • *title, author/director, year, length (pages/minutes), setting*<br>• *basic information: genre/type of movie/book (action, drama, comedy), characters, one-sentence summary of plot* |
| *Main part* | • *short summary of the plot (but don't reveal too much!)*<br>• *more information about characters (and cast if you're writing about a movie)* |
| *Conclusion* | • *your opinion, e. g. on characters, plot, actors, dialogue, special effects, the message of the book/movie, …*<br>• *recommendation; who is the target group? (e. g. young adults, comedy fans, people who like drama/romance)* |

**TIPP:** Verwende starke Adjektive und Adverbien, um deine Leser entweder von dem Buch/Film zu überzeugen oder abzuschrecken (an **action-packed** thriller, a **hilarious** comedy, a **highly** entertaining movie, a **boring** drama with **one-dimensional** characters …).

## 13 Writing a summary ➜ *SB (p. 172)*

PLANUNGSPHASE

**Step 1:** Lies den Text genau. Mach dir Notizen (➜ *SMC 41*) oder markiere wichtige Stellen im Text (➜ *SMC 2*).

**Step 2:** Beantworte die *wh*-Fragen **Who? What? Where? When? Why?** zum Text. Du kannst dir Stichwörter am Rand machen.

**Who?** *Who does something? Who is the text about?*
**What?** *What happens? What does person X do?*
**Where?** *Where does it take place?*
**When?** *When does it take place?*
**Why?** *Why does person X act this way?*
*Why does something happen?*

**Step 3:** Entscheide, welche Textteile wichtige Informationen enthalten. Beispiele, Vergleiche, direkte Rede oder Zahlen und Ähnliches gehören nicht in eine Zusammenfassung.

SCHREIBPHASE

**Step 1:** Schreib einen ersten Entwurf deiner Zusammenfassung:

- Beginne mit einer Einleitung, in der wichtige Informationen wie Titel, Autor/in, Thema und Hauptaussage des Textes stehen. Wenn du einen Zeitungsartikel zusammenfasst, solltest du hier auch die Quelle nennen.
- Verwende immer das **simple present**. Ausnahme hiervon: Wenn der Autor etwas beschreibt, das in der Vergangenheit oder der Zukunft liegt, z. B. in einem Zeitungsartikel, kannst du das auch so wiedergeben. Beispiel:
  *The writer **describes** the festival in New York, which **started** on Saturday, 4th April.*
- Kopiere den Text nicht, sondern benutze deine eigenen Worte.

**Step 2:** Überarbeite deine Zusammenfassung:

- Hast du alle wichtigen Aspekte genannt?
- Hast du unwichtige Details weggelassen?
- Ist dein Text durchgängig im *simple present* (außer in den genannten Ausnahmen)?
- Hast du deine Textteile gut verbunden? Ist dein Text logisch aufgebaut und gut zu verstehen?
- Vergiss auch nicht, den Text auf Rechtschreibung und Zeichensetzung zu checken. (➜ *SMC 14, 15*)

**LANGUAGE HELP:**
Folgende *phrases* können dir bei der Einleitung helfen:
- *The story/text is about …*
- *The text deals with …*
- *The article/text shows …*

## 14 Revising texts ➜ *SB (p. 173)*

TEXTÜBERARBEITUNG

1 Stimmt die Struktur?
Jeder Text braucht
- eine Einleitung, die in das Thema einführt,
- einen Hauptteil, der das Thema ausführt,
- einen Schluss, der alles auf den Punkt bringt. (➜ *SMC 3*)

2 Stimmt der Aufbau der Absätze?
Jeder Absatz
- befasst sich mit einem zusammenhängenden Gedanken,
- beginnt mit einem ***topic sentence***, der diesen Gedanken einführt. (➜ *SMC 3*)

3 Stimmen die Verknüpfungen?
Gute *linking words*
- schaffen Verbindungen zwischen Sätzen oder Satzteilen,
- helfen, Zusammenhänge verständlich zu machen. (➜ *SMC 4*)

4 Sind die Zeitangaben richtig gesetzt?
*Time markers*
- helfen, sich z. B. in einer Geschichte zurechtzufinden,
- machen das Geschehen anschaulicher. (➜ *SMC 4*)

5 Enthält der Text Adjektive und Adverbien?
Adjektive und Adverbien
- erlauben nähere Beschreibungen von Personen und Dingen,
- machen Texte anschaulicher. (➜ *SMC 4*)

6 Hat der Text sprachliche/grammatikalische Fehler?
Überprüfe deinen Text
- auf Rechtschreibung und Satzzeichen,
- auf grammatische Formen, z. B. Verbformen, Satzbau (*word order*) usw.

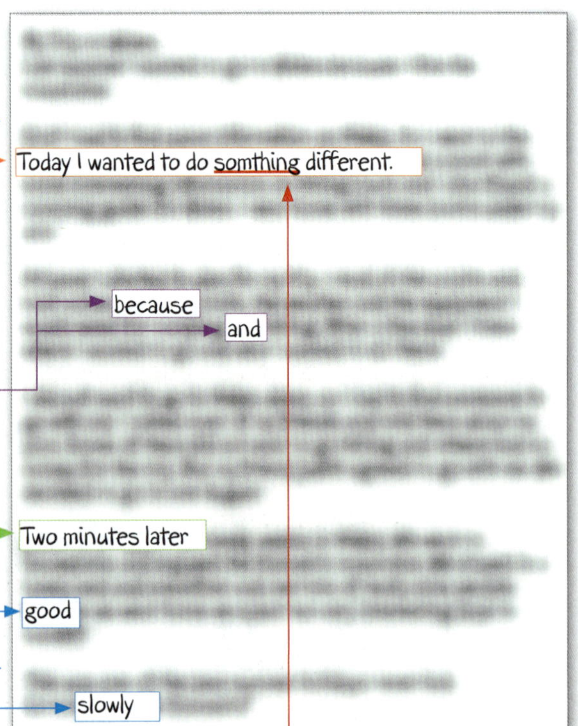

## 15 Revising and improving electronic texts ➜ *SB (p. 174)*

Viele deiner Texte schreibst du nicht mit der Hand, sondern am Computer, sei es für eine Hausaufgabe, ein Referat oder ein Projekt.

Bei der Überarbeitung dieser Texte gelten dieselben Grundsätze wie beim Überarbeiten aller Texte (➜ *SMC 14*), aber es kommen auch noch ein paar Besonderheiten dazu. Diese findest du im Folgenden:

### KORREKTUR

- Nutze die Überprüfungsfunktion deines Textverarbeitungsprogramms. Aber: sieh dir alle gemeldeten Fehler genau an, denn nicht alles, was als falsch angezeigt wird, ist auch wirklich falsch.
- Lies deinen Text trotz der Überprüfung durch das Programm noch einmal Korrektur, denn nicht alle Fehler werden auch als solche erkannt (z. B. wenn ein Tippfehler zu einem anderen korrekten Wort führt, das aber im Kontext nicht passt wie *the* ***win*** *in the trees* statt *the* ***wind*** *in the trees*).

**TIPP:** Wichtig: Denk dran, vor der Überprüfung deines Textes die Rechtschreibüberprüfung auf „Englisch (Großbritannien)" einzustellen.

### LAYOUT

- Lass genügend Abstand an den **Rändern** (normalerweise reichen die voreingestellten Ränder in deinem Textverarbeitungsprogramm, also 2,5 cm).
- Richte den Text **linksbündig** aus, denn das ist am besten lesbar (Ausnahme: die Überschrift kann zentriert sein, ebenso wie z. B. ein Zitat zum Einstieg).
- **Zwischenüberschriften** lockern den Text auf und machen das Lesen leichter, weil sie größere Textblöcke unterteilen.
- Überlege dir gut, wo du **Bilder** einbaust und welche Größe sie haben sollen: Bilder, die einen Inhalt im Text veranschaulichen, sollten auch möglichst nah an dieser Textstelle platziert werden. Die Größe solltest du so wählen, dass der Inhalt gut zu erkennen ist. Gib immer die **Quelle** an, wenn du ein Bild verwendest, v. a. wenn möglich auch den Namen des Urhebers/der Urheberin. (➜ *SMC 27, 28, 29*)

**TIPP:** Wenn dein Text der Öffentlichkeit zugänglich gemacht wird, z. B. auf der Schulwebseite, musst du vor der Verwendung von Bildern die Urheber um Erlaubnis fragen. (➜ *SMC 27, 28, 29*)

### ZITATE

Wenn du Zitate verwendet hast, überprüfe, ob sie als solche erkennbar sind:

- Sind sie in **Anführungszeichen** gesetzt?
- Hast du die **Quelle des Zitats** angegeben?
- Ist der **Wortlaut des Zitats** genau wie im Original? Wenn nicht, hast du Auslassungen kenntlich gemacht? (➜ *SMC 10*)

### FORMATIERUNG

- Wähle eine gut lesbare **Schriftart**. Benutze diese Schrift für den kompletten Text. Für Überschriften oder Bildunterschriften kannst du eine andere Schrift verwenden (aber nie mehr als drei verscheidene Schriftarten).
- Die **Schriftgröße** sollte so groß sein, dass der Text gut lesbar ist (z. B. 12 pt). Das gilt auch für den **Zeilenabstand**.
- Zur Hervorhebung bestimmter Textstellen, z. B. Zitaten, Songtiteln, Buchtiteln, Namen etc., kannst du **Schriftstile** wie **fett**, *kursiv* oder unterstrichen verwenden. Du solltest aber sparsam damit umgehen, damit der Text nicht unübersichtlich wird und auch nicht alles gleichzeitig verwenden.

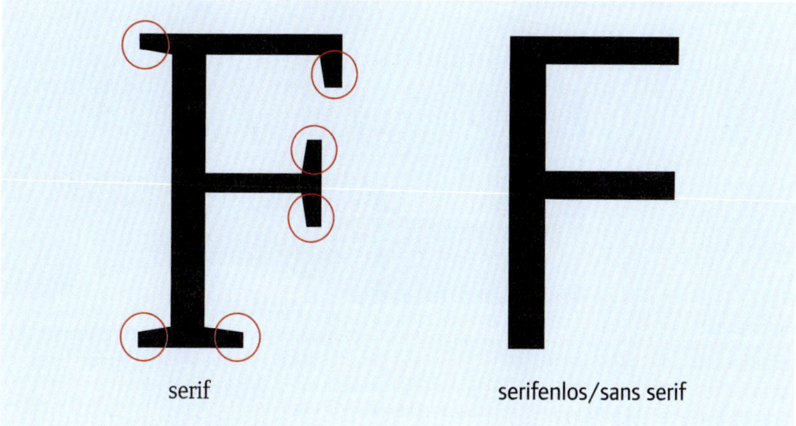


**TIPP:** Bei **Schriften** unterscheidet man zwischen **serifen** (z. B. Times New Roman) und **serifenlosen** (z. B. Arial). Für **längere, gedruckte Texte** nimmt man in der Regel serife Schriften. **Kürzere Texte** und solche, die vor allem am Bildschirm gelesen, wirken durch serifenlose Schriften oft lesbarer.

## 16 Mediating written or spoken information ➔ *SB (p. 175)*

Wenn du Informationen in einer anderen Sprache wiedergeben sollst, geht es nicht darum, alles zu übersetzen, sondern es kommt darauf an, die wichtigsten Informationen herauszusuchen.

### Schriftliche Informationen

- **Scanne** den Text gezielt nach den geforderten Informationen. (➔ *SMC 1*)
- Mach dir keine Sorgen, wenn du nicht jedes Wort verstehst. Das ist oft nicht nötig, um die wichtigen Punkte zu erfassen.
- Wenn der Text länger ist und du viele Informationen im Blick behalten musst, **markiere** die wichtigsten Textstellen. (➔ *SMC 2*)
- Mach dir **Notizen** in deinen eigenen Worten. (➔ *SMC 41*)

### Mündliche Informationen

- Achte beim Hören gezielt auf die gesuchten Informationen. (➔ *SMC 26*)
- Mach dir Notizen (➔ *SMC 41*)
- Überlege, wie du deine Notizen am besten in der anderen Sprache wiedergeben kannst.

**TIPP:** Bei **Mediation im Unterricht** hast du in der Regel eine Aufgabenstellung, die dir sagt, worauf du beim Lesen oder Hören achten musst bzw. welche Stellen du wiedergeben sollst.
Konzentriere dich beim Lesen auf diese Stellen *(scanning)* bzw. mach dir gezielt Notizen.

**TIPP:** Wenn du den Inhalt eines Textes schriftlich in einer anderen Sprache wiedergeben sollst, achte darauf, dass deine Mediation nicht länger ist als ca. 35–40 % des Originaltextes. (➔ *SMC 13*)

## 17 Selecting relevant information ➔ *SB (p. 175)*

Manchmal gibt es keine gezielten Fragen oder Aufgabenstellungen dazu, welche Informationen du aus einem Text heraussuchen sollst. In der Regel hast du aber trotzdem Anhaltspunkte, die sich aus der Situation ergeben oder aus dem, was dir dein Gegenüber erzählt hat.
Wenn du in einer solchen Situation bist, helfen folgende Hinweise:

- **Analysiere die Situation**, um abzuschätzen, um welche Informationen es gehen könnte (Restaurant, Bahnhof, Flughafen usw.).
- Wenn du unsicher bist, **frage nach**.
- **Übersetze** wichtige Stichworte direkt, wenn du die Wörter kennst.
- **Umschreibe Begriffe**, die du nicht kennst.

**TIPP:** Wenn du Informationen wiedergibst, kannst du oft Details zu einem Begriff zusammenfassen. Wenn z. B. in einem Text *Twitter, Facebook, tumblr* und *Pinterest* vorkommen, kannst du *social media* sagen, anstatt alle aufzuzählen.

## 18 Paraphrasing ➔ *SB (p. 176)*

Es fällt dir eventuell manchmal schwer, mündliche Aussagen oder Texte in Englisch wiederzugeben, z. B. weil

- dein Wortschatz nicht ausreicht
- dir bekannte Wörter „im Stress" der Situation nicht einfallen
- oder spezielle Fachbegriffe auftauchen.

Wenn dir das passiert, dann solltest du versuchen, diese Wörter zu umschreiben, z. B. mithilfe von Relativsätzen:

*It's somebody/a person who*
*It's something that you use to …*
*It's an animal that*
*It's a place that/where …*

**TIPP:** Oft helfen beim Umschreiben auch **Synonyme** (gleiche Bedeutung) oder **Antonyme** (gegenteilige Bedeutung).
Wenn du die weißt, kannst du z. B. sagen:
- *It's the same as …*
- *It's the opposite of …*

## 19 Cultural differences ➔ *SB (p. 176)*

Wenn du anderen Menschen hilfst, Texte oder Gehörtes zu verstehen, kann es neben Wortschatzproblemen auch noch andere Schwierigkeiten geben. Diese sind häufig in **kulturellen Unterschieden** begründet.
Dinge, die häufig zu **Missverständnissen** führen, sind z. B.

- **Temperaturen:** 30 Grad bei uns sind heiß, aber in den USA eher kalt, weil dort Temperaturen in Fahrenheit angegeben werden.
- **Längenangaben/Geschwindigkeit:** Bei uns wird das metrische System verwendet (Meter, Kilometer usw.), in den USA das *imperial system* mit *inch, yard* und *mile.* 75 mph (Meilen pro Stunde) sind z. B. ca. 120 km/h.

Wenn du feststellst, dass es zu einem Missverständnis gekommen ist, kannst du folgende Dinge probieren:

- Frage höflich nach, wo das Missverständnis liegt und versuche, es durch eine neue Erklärung zu beseitigen.
- Ergänze deine Erläuterung evtl. mit **Hintergrundinformationen:** Es kann sein, dass du bestimmte Dinge, die für dich völlig normal sind, erklären musst (z. B. Mülltrennung oder das Benutzen des Nahverkehrs).
- Sei offen für die Erklärungen, die du im Gegenzug bekommst – hierbei kannst du Dinge über das Land deines Gegenübers lernen.

## 20 Communicating in everyday situations ➔ *SB (p. 177)*

Es ist nicht immer einfach, sich mit Menschen aus anderen Ländern zu unterhalten. Neben der Sprachbarriere gibt es oft kulturelle Unterschiede. Die folgenden Schritte helfen dir, wenn du dich flüssig unterhalten willst:

**Step 1:** Beginne freundlich, z. B. mit etwas, was euch verbindet (der Ort, die Situation usw.).

**Step 2:** Halte das Gespräch am Laufen:
- Zeige dein Interesse, indem du Fragen stellst.
- Vermeide einsilbige Antworten, um nicht desinteressiert oder unfreundlich zu wirken.
- Wenn du etwas nicht verstehst, frage nach.
- Wenn du etwas nicht sagen kannst, versuche es zu umschreiben oder bitte deinen Gesprächspartner um Hilfe.

**Step 3:** Beende das Gespräch so freundlich, wie du es angefangen hast:
- Bedanke dich, wenn du um Hilfe gebeten hast.
- Verabschiede dich freundlich.

## 21 Having a discussion ➔ *SB (p. 178)*

In einer Diskussion tauscht man Meinungen und Ideen zu einem bestimmten Thema aus.

### VORBEREITUNGSPHASE

**Step 1:** Bereite dich vor: Recherchiere Fakten und Beispiele. Überlege, was deine Meinung zu dem Thema ist. Mach dir Notizen.

**Step 2:** Halte deine Notizen für die Diskussion bereit, z. B. auf kleinen Zetteln.

**Step 3:** Überlege dir vorher ein Statement, das deine Meinung zum Thema gut ausdrückt.

### DISKUSSION

**Step 1:** **Starting the discussion:** Sag deine Meinung (z. B. mithilfe der Eröffnung, die du dir überlegt hast).

**Step 2:** **Continuing the discussion:** Tausch deine Meinung mit anderen aus. Bleib höflich und sachlich. Hör den anderen zu und lass sie ausreden.
- Wenn du sprichst, bezieh dich auf die anderen und sag, weshalb du ihren Argumenten zustimmst (oder nicht).
- Stütz deine Meinung mit Fakten und Beispielen.

**Step 3:** **Ending the discussion:**
- Fass deinen Standpunkt noch einmal knapp zusammen.
- Versucht, Gemeinsamkeiten festzustellen, oder einigt euch darüber, dass es keine gemeinsame Lösung gibt *(agree to disagree).*
- Falls gefordert, einigt euch auf eine Lösung oder einen Kompromiss.

**TIPP:** Bei Rollenspielen musst du manchmal eine Meinung vertreten, die anders ist als deine eigene. Dann kannst du in deinen Notizen z. B. versuchen, Argumente und Gegenargumente einander gegenüberzustellen, um in der Diskussion schnell und gut reagieren zu können.

**TIPP:** Im Englischen ist man häufig weit weniger direkt als im Deutschen. Das bedeutet, dass du bei Diskussionen
- besonders gut zuhören musst, weil du sonst evtl. nicht genau mitbekommst, ob man dir zustimmt oder widersprichst;
- kurze, zu direkte Antworten wie *"No."* vermeiden solltest, weil sie unhöflich wirken.

## 22 Agreeing and disagreeing with people's opinions ➔ *SB (p. 178)*

Es ist bei Diskussionen hilfreich, einige Redewendungen parat zu haben.
Dann kannst du dich auf deine Argumente konzentrieren.

LANGUAGE HELP: Folgende Phrasen solltest du dir aufschreiben und lernen:

| Stating your opinion | Agreeing | Disagreeing |
|---|---|---|
| *In my opinion …* | *I agree …* | *I'm afraid I don't quite agree …* |
| *Well, I'd say …* | *Exactly./Absolutely./…* | *I'm not sure about that.* |
| *It's a fact that …* | *You're quite right.* | *Do you really think so?* |
| *Personally, I think…* | *I think so too.* | *I'm not convinced that …* |
| *If you ask me …* | *You've got a good point there.* | *I doubt that (very much).* |
| *I think/feel/believe …* | *That's exactly how I see it.* | *I don't agree with you at all.* |
| *First of all, I'd like to point out …* | *That's true/right.* | *I disagree (completely).* |
| *I'm certain that …* | *I couldn't agree with you more.* | *It's not as simple as that.* |

## 23 Preparing and taking part in a panel discussion ➔ *SB (p. 179)*

### VORBEREITUNGSPHASE

**Step 1:** Recherchiere Fakten und überlege, was deine Meinung zu dem Thema ist. Mache dir Notizen.

**Step 2:** Halte deine Notizen für die Diskussion bereit – z. B. auf kleinen Zetteln – damit du darauf zugreifen kannst, falls du sie brauchst.

**Step 3:** Bereite dich in der Diskussion vor – Moderator, Diskussionsteilnehmer oder Zuhörer. Jede Rolle hat andere Aufgaben. Nützliche Redemittel (➔ *SMC 22*) können auf einem **discussion fan** notiert werden, damit sie schnell zur Hand sind.

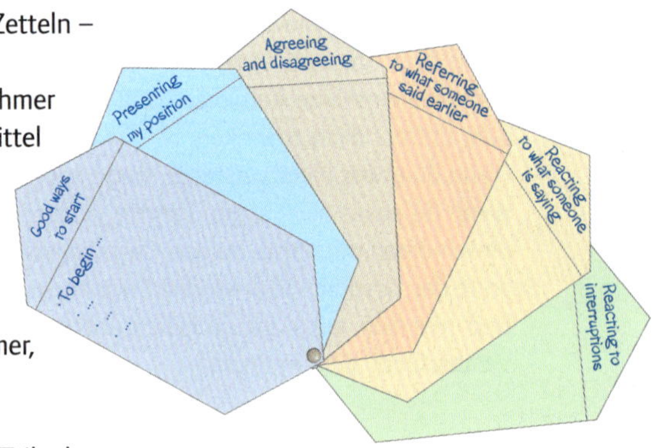


### MODERATOR/IN

Die Moderatorin/Der Moderator einer Podiumsdiskussion
- überlegt sich im Vorfeld der Diskussion mögliche Fragen für die Teilnehmer,
- stellt kurz die Diskussionsteilnehmer vor,
- leitet die Diskussion und stellt Fragen, wenn die Diskussion stockt,
- sorgt dafür, dass sich alle Beteiligten an die Regeln halten und dass alle Teilnehmer etwa gleich viel Redezeit haben,
- achtet auf die Zeit oder bestimmt einen ***timekeeper***, der dies tut,
- ermuntert die Zuhörer, Fragen zu stellen und moderiert diese.

### DISKUSSIONSTEILNEHMER/IN

Die Teilnehmer einer Podiumsdiskussion
- sind gut vorbereitet: sie haben sich ihre eigenen Argumente notiert und sich Gedanken zu den möglichen Argumenten der anderen Teilnehmer gemacht,
- geben zu Beginn der Diskussion ein kurzes Statement, das ihre Meinung knapp zusammenfasst,
- folgen der Diskussion aufmerksam und notieren sich Argumente der anderen Teilnehmer, um darauf reagieren zu können.

### ZUHÖRER/IN

Die Zuhörer bei einer Podiumsdiskussion
- überlegen sich im Vorfeld, welche Argumente sie zu bestimmten Themen erwarten und überlegen sich entsprechende Fragen/Kommentare,
- können sich im Anschluss an die Diskussion dazu äußern, welche Argumente sie am überzeugendsten fanden,
- machen sich während der Diskussion Notizen, um im Anschluss Fragen zu stellen oder die Argumente kommentieren zu können.

### DURCHFÜHRUNG

Eine Podiumsdiskussion sollte einen vorher vereinbarten Zeitrahmen nicht überschreiten. Im Anschluss daran sollte Zeit für Fragen und Kommentare der Zuhörer eingeplant werden.

## 24 Taking part in an interview ➔ *SB (p. 180)*

Bei Bewerbungsgesprächen helfen die folgenden 4 Ps:

### PREPARE

- Finde so viel wie möglich über den Job und den Arbeitgeber heraus.
- Notiere mögliche Fragen, die du dem Arbeitgeber stellen kannst.
- Überleg dir aber auch, welche Fragen man dir stellen könnte, und bereite Antworten darauf vor.

### PRACTISE

- Übe das Bewerbungsgespräch mit einem Partner/einer Partnerin.
- Gib deinem Partner/deiner Partnerin die Fragen, die du von deinem Arbeitgeber erwartest, und beantworte sie. Sag ihm/ihr auch, dass er/sie dir ruhig unerwartete Fragen stellen soll. So übst du, darauf zu antworten.

### PRESENT

- Überleg dir, was du zu dem Bewerbungsgespräch anziehen möchtest. Die Auswahl der Kleidung hängt vom Arbeitgeber ab.
- Stell sicher, dass du pünktlich bist. Finde vorher heraus, wie du zum Ort des Gesprächs kommst. Plane Zeit für Unvorhergesehenes ein. Es ist immer besser, zehn Minuten zu früh als zu spät zu sein.

### PARTICIPATE

- Stell dich am Anfang vor und lächle dabei freundlich.
- Lass dir Zeit, Fragen zu beantworten, besonders wenn es unerwartete Fragen sind. Antworte nicht mit *"Yes."* oder *"No."*, sondern versuche, Fragen ausführlich und höflich zu beantworten.
- Wenn du eine Frage nicht verstehst, frag nach.
- Verabschiede dich am Ende des Gesprächs mit einem freundlichen Lächeln und bedanke dich.

**TIPP:** Achte auch auf deine nonverbale Kommunikation – wie du stehst, gehst, sitzt – und sieh deinem Gegenüber in die Augen.

## 25 Viewing ➔ *SB (p. 181)*

Es gibt viele Elemente, die die Atmosphäre und die **Wirkung** eines Films beeinflussen:

- **Genre:** Handelt es sich um einen Dokumentarfilm **(documentary)**, einen Spielfilm **(feature film)** wie z. B. **thriller, science-fiction/sci-fi movie, comedy** oder ein **drama**? Oder ist es ein Videoclip oder ein Werbefilm?
- **Story:** Wo und wann spielt der Film **(setting)**? Besetzung der Rollen **(cast)**, Schauplatz **(location)**, Handlung **(plot)**.
- **Camera:** Erst durch die Bilder der **Kamera** ist der Zuschauer in der Lage, einen Film wahrzunehmen. Die Kamera stellt das Blickfeld her und begrenzt es gleichzeitig, z. B. hinsichtlich der Beziehung der Charaktere zueinander. Auch die Stimmung oder Spannung in einer Szene wird von der Kameraführung beeinflusst. Dafür gibt es z. B. folgende Mittel:
  - **Shots:** Die **Kameraeinstellung** beeinflusst, wie man Szenen wahrnimmt, ob z. B. Personen oder Objekte als Nahaufnahme **(close-up)**, aus der mittleren Distanz **(medium shot)** oder als Totale **(long shot)** gefilmt sind.
  - **Editing:** Filme werden in der Regel nicht chronologisch gedreht und auch nicht nur mit einer einzigen Kamera, d. h. am Ende der Dreharbeiten müssen viele einzelne Shots zusammengefügt werden. Dieser **Filmschnitt** bestimmt, wie eine Szene wirkt. Er bestimmt auch den Rhythmus – lange Einstellungen mit wenigen Schnitten wirken eher ruhig, können aber auch große Spannung erzeugen, während schnelle, harte Schnitte eher actiongeladen wirken.
- **Soundtrack:** Die **Musik** in eine Szene hat großen Einfluss darauf, wie man die Szene wahrnimmt. Eine Actionszene wird meist mit schneller, lauter Musik unterlegt, eine romantische Szene eher mit ruhiger, leiser Musik. Dies verstärkt die Wirkung des Gesehenen.

## 26 Listening strategies ➔ *SB (pp. 182–183)*

### LISTENING FOR DETAIL

- Überleg dir vorher, auf welche Informationen du achten musst.
  - Bei einem Wetterbericht sind das z. B. Beschreibungen wie *sunny, cloudy, chance of rain* etc., bei Bahnhofsansagen z. B. Wörter wie *platform* oder Orte und Zeiten.
  - Höre dann gezielt auf solche Wörter und notiere sie. (➔ *SMC 41*)
- Manchmal können dir Signalwörter helfen, dem Inhalt zu folgen:
  - Gründe, Folgen: *because, so, so that, …*
  - Vergleiche: *larger/older/… than, as … as, more, most, …*
  - Reihenfolge: *before, after, then, next, later, …*

### LISTENING FOR GIST

- Mach dir keine Sorgen, wenn du nicht jedes Wort verstehst – das brauchst du nicht, um dem Inhalt oberflächlich folgen zu können. Überlege dir anhand der Aufgabe, um was es gehen könnte, und konzentriere dich darauf.
- Versuch, von den Aussagen, die du verstehst, auf Inhalte zu schließen, die noch kommen könnten.

**TIPP:** Im Unterricht kannst du Texte oft zweimal hören und hast weitere Hilfen:

- Sieh dir die Aufgabenstellung an: Was sollst du heraushören?
- Sieh dir Titel und Bilder an.
- Vergleiche nach dem Hören mit einem Partner/einer Partnerin, was ihr verstanden habt.
- Vervollständige deine Notizen sofort.

## 27 Finding information online ➔ *SB (pp. 183–184)*

- Überleg, was die wichtigsten **Stichwörter** für dein Thema sind. Für das Thema „The Beatles in Hamburg" wären *Beatles* und *Hamburg* ein guter Start.
- Gib deine Stichwörter in eine **Suchmaschine** ein. Je mehr gute Stichwörter du eingibst, desto genauer sind die Ergebnisse. In der Infografik rechts kannst du sehen, wie du an ganz spezielle Informationen kommen kannst.
- Verwende möglichst Suchmaschinen, die deine Suchen nicht tracken, um deine Privatsphäre zu schützen.
- Sieh dir mehrere **Suchergebnisse** an, um zu prüfen, ob sie passen. Wenn du schnell ein bestimmtes Wort wie *Hamburg* finden willst, dann kannst du mit der Tastenkombination ***Strg + F*** (Mac: Cmd + F) danach suchen. Das Wort wird dann auf der Seite markiert und du kannst schnell sehen, ob die Information relevant ist.
- Achte darauf, wer die Webseite erstellt hat, um die **Qualität** der Suchergebnisse einzuschätzen. Sind sie wohl zuverlässig (Online-Lexikon, bekannte Medien) oder eher persönliche Meinungen (Forum, Fan-Seite ...)?
- Kopiere nicht einfach ganze Artikel aus dem Internet. Mach dir Notizen und verwende deine eigenen Worte, um die Inhalte wiederzugeben.
- Setz dir ein Zeitlimit für deine Recherche und ordne dann dein Material. Prüfe, ob dir etwas fehlt, und such ggf. gezielt nur noch nach diesen Informationen.
- Leg alle interessanten Materialien zu deinem Thema in einem eigenen Ordner ab. Dann kannst du sie dir später genauer ansehen und auswählen, was du nutzen möchtest.

**Internet research**
**Tipps und Tricks**

Wenn du ganz spezifische Informationen suchst, helfen diese Tricks:

**Was du suchst:** Artikel aus der *Wikipedia*, in denen du Informationen über die Zeit der Beatles in Hamburg findest.

**Wie du danach suchst:**

site: wikipidia.com "the beatles" "hamburg"

| **site:** | **" "** |
|---|---|
| sucht nur auf der genannten Seite | sucht die exakten Begriffe und erzwingt das Vorkommen im Suchergebnis |

**Was du suchst:** Einen englischsprachigen Bericht, am liebsten als PDF, über den Lebensraum von Füchsen.

**Wie du danach suchst:**

filetype:pdf intitle:habitat of *fox

| **filetype:** | **intitle:** | * |
|---|---|---|
| sucht nur diesen Dateityp (pdf, doc, jpg usw.) | zeigt nur Ergebnisse, in denen dieses Wort im Titel auftaucht | sucht auch Worte wie Red Fox, Black Fox, Desert Fox usw. |

**TIPP:** Du kannst bei einfachen Suchanfragen auch direkt die Frage ins Suchfeld eingeben, z. B. *What is 20 oz in grams?* Die Suchmaschine sucht sich dann selbst die relevanten Stichworte heraus – hier *20 oz* und *grams* – und liefert die Antwort. Bei komplexeren Suchanfragen sind die Antworten oft besser, je genauere Suchbegriffe du dir überlegst.

## 28 Creating a good layout for a page or poster ➔ *SB (p. 185)*

- Sortiere die **Informationen**, die du vermitteln willst: Was ist wichtig? Was ist ein Unterpunkt? Hast du Beispiele für Thesen/Argumente?
- Gib deinem Produkt eine klare **Struktur**: Texte haben meist drei Teile (Einleitung, Hauptteil, Schluss), während Poster häufig aus Aufzählungen wichtiger Punkte bestehen.
- Beginne für jeden neuen Gedanken einen neuen Absatz bzw. einen neuen Stichpunkt.
- Eine **Überschrift** verdeutlicht, worum es in deinem Text geht. Wenn es in deinem Produkt um mehrere Themen geht, dann kannst du für einzelne Abschnitte auch **Zwischenüberschriften** verwenden. Das gibt dem Ganzen eine klare Struktur und hilft den Lesenden, sich schnell zu orientieren.
- Ergänze dein Produkt mit **passenden Fotos, Videos, Audios, Statistiken** etc. Vergiss nicht anzugeben, woher die Medien stammen (➔ *SMC 27, 29*)
- Wenn nicht auf den ersten Blick erkennbar ist, was ein Bild zeigt, füge **Bildunterschriften** ein.
- Formatiere dein Produkt so, dass es gut lesbar ist. Dabei ist das Medium wichtig – für einen ausgedruckten Handzettel kannst du andere **Schriftarten** wählen als für einen Text, der am Bildschirm gelesen wird. (➔ *SMC 23*) Für ein Poster (z. B. für einen *gallery walk*) muss die **Schriftgröße** größer sein als für einen Ausdruck. Eine große Schrift hilft dir auch, nicht zu viele Punkte auf dem Poster unterzubringen – hier ist weniger mehr.

## 29 Making good slides for an electronic presentation ➔ *SB (pp. 185–186)*

TEXT

- Verwende möglichst wenige Folien.
- Nutze **Aufzählungen** mit *keywords*, keine ganzen Sätze, und schreibe nicht mehr als sechs Zeilen auf eine Folie.
- Wähle eine ausreichende **Schriftgröße** (mindestens 30 pt, gerne mehr) und eine gut lesbare Schrift. Lass einen ausreichend großen **Abstand** zwischen den Zeilen.
- Richte den **Text linksbündig** aus, außer du verfolgst ein ganz besonderes Ziel damit (z. B. zentriert zum Herausheben eines Zitats), aber mische die Ausrichtung nicht auf einer Folie.

ABBILDUNGEN

- Manche Inhalte kannst du gut nur mit einem passenden Bild oder einer Grafik statt mit Worten ausdrücken.
- Suche ein Bild, dass die Aussage deines Vortrags verdeutlicht, z. B. ein Foto, das ein Problem gut darstellt. Manchmal eignet sich auch eine Grafik, z. B. ein Diagramm.
- Wichtig: Bei allen Bildern, die du verwendest, musst du die Quelle angeben, d. h. den Fotografen/die Fotografin, den Illustrator/die Illustratorin etc. sowie den Ort, wo du das Bild gefunden hast. (Eine Suchmaschine ist keine Quellenangabe!)

## 30 Giving a presentation ➜ SB (p. 186)

**Wie halte ich eine gute Präsentation?**

### VORBEREITUNG

- Sammle Informationen zu deinem Thema.
- Wähle eine Form der Präsentation aus, die das Thema gut veranschaulicht (Poster, Folie, Tafel, ...).
- Mach dir Notizen, z. B. auf nummerierten Karteikarten oder in einer App.
- Bereite deine Medien vor (Poster, Folie, Tafelanschrieb, ...). Schreibe groß und für alle gut lesbar.
- Übe deine Präsentation zu Hause vor einem Spiegel oder vor einem kleinen Publikum (Eltern, Großeltern, Freunde).
- Sprich laut, deutlich und langsam.

### DURTCHFÜHRUNG

- Warte, bis es ruhig ist. Schaue die Zuhörer/innen an.
- Beginne mit einem prägnanten Einstieg, z. B. einem Zitat oder einer Frage, die das Interesse der Zuhörer weckt.
- Erkläre, worüber du sprechen wirst und wie deine Präsentation aufgebaut ist.
- Lies nicht von deinen Karten ab, sondern sprich möglichst frei.
- Erkläre unbekannten Wortschatz, besonders, wenn er zum Verständnis deines Themas wichtig ist.

### SCHLUSS

- Komme am Ende noch einmal auf deinen Einstieg zurück, indem du z. B. die Frage aus dem Einstieg wieder aufgreifst und beantwortest.
- Bei längeren Präsentation solltest du am Ende die wichtigsten Punkte noch einmal zusammenfassen und das Wichtigste herausheben.
- Bedanke dich am Ende fürs Zuhören.
- Frag die Zuhörer/innen, ob sie Fragen haben und beantworte diese.

## 31 Talking about statistics ➜ SB (p. 187)

Wenn du Statistiken analysieren und vorstellen sollst, gehst du am besten wie folgt vor:

**Step 1:** Identifiziere, welche Art von Diagramm du vor dir hast – **pie chart**, **bar chart**, **line graph** oder **Tabelle** – und sieh dir die Quelle an:
- Ist die Quelle verlässlich?
- Sind die Angaben/Zahlen im Diagramm aktuell?

**Step 2:** Beschreibe das Diagramm/die Tabelle:
- Worum geht es? Welche Informationen gibt das Diagramm?
  *The bar chart / pie chart / line graph / table / ... shows the different ... / compares the size / number of ... / is about ... / contrasts ... with ...*
- Zeigen die Daten eine Entwicklung oder werden verschiedene Zeitpunkte miteinander verglichen?
  *It shows ... in contrast to ...*
  *The chart gives us information about who/what/how many/...*
- Werden absolute Zahlen oder Prozentangaben verwendet?
  *The chart/table shows us the number of / percentage of ...*
  *It shows which percentage of ...*

**Step 3:** Ziehe deine Schlussfolgerungen aus dem Diagramm / der Tabelle:
*My main conclusion is that ...*
*The most important thing I've learned is that ...*
*One thing that I hadn't realized before is ...*

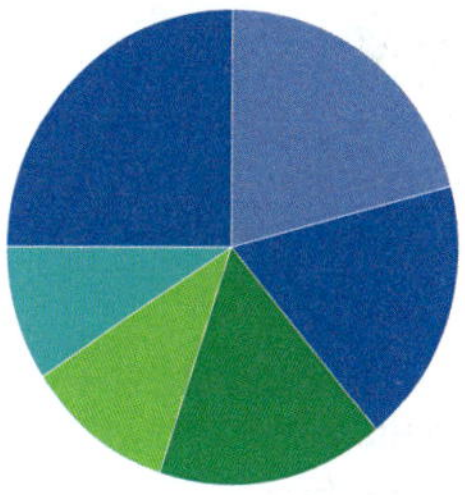

*pie chart*

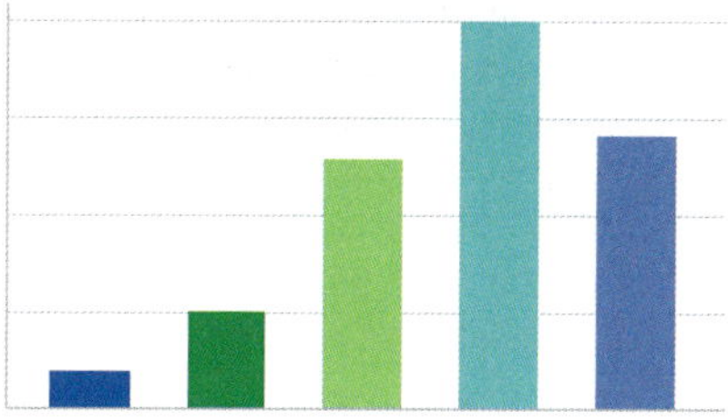

*bar chart*

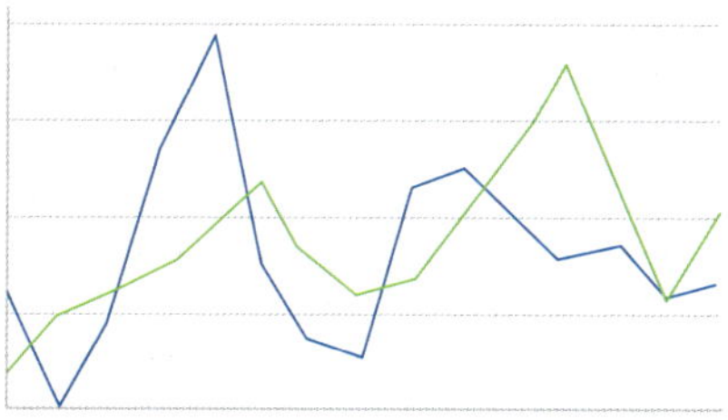

*line graph*

## 32 Describing and presenting pictures ➜ *SB (p. 188)*

Manchmal sollst du ein Foto vor der Klasse vorstellen und es dabei beschreiben. Hier sind ein paar Hilfen.

**Wie stelle ich ein Foto vor?**

1 Stelle das Foto vor und sage, woher es kommt.

2 Beschreibe das Foto:
- Sage, was wo zu sehen ist: *at the top/bottom* · *in the foreground/background* · *in the middle* · *on the left/right*
- Diese Präpositionen sind auch hilfreich: *behind* · *between* · *in front of* · *next to* · *under* · *over*
- Geh bei der Beschreibung in einer bestimmten Reihenfolge vor, z. B. von links nach rechts oder von oben nach unten.

3 Sage, was dir an dem Foto gefällt oder nicht.

4 Wenn du mit der Vorstellung des Fotos fertig bist, bedanke dich fürs Zuhören und frage, ob noch jemand Fragen hat.

**1** *I'd like to talk about this photo of … I found it on the internet / in a magazine / …*

**2** *In the foreground you can see … I think the people in the photo are talking about … / having fun / celebrating / …*

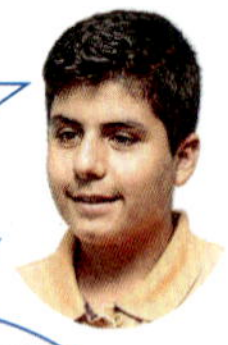

**3** *I really like/don't like the photo because … It's interesting/boring/exciting/… because …*

**4** *Thank you for listening. Do you have any questions?*

## 33 Working in a team ➜ *SB (p. 188)*

Bei Projekten arbeitet ihr oft im Team. Dabei solltet ihr eure unterschiedlichen Fähigkeiten und Talente einbringen und bestimmte Regeln beachten. Folgende Schritte können helfen, die Arbeit zu organisieren:

**Step 1:** Legt **Regeln** für die Arbeit in der Gruppe fest, z. B. gegenseitige Unterstützung, pünktliches und zügiges Arbeiten, einander zuhören oder verschiedene Lösungen diskutieren usw.

**Step 2:** Sammelt Ideen für die Bearbeitung eures Themas (z. B. in einer Mindmap). Wählt gemeinsam Unterthemen aus und legt die **Arbeitsschritte** fest, die für die Bearbeitung nötig sind.

**Step 3:** Verteilt **Rollen** und Aufgaben nach euren Interessen und Fähigkeiten. Wenn ihr euch nicht einigen könnt, hilft Auslosen oder Würfeln. Folgende Rollen solltet ihr auf jeden Fall verteilen:
- coordinator
- writer
- researcher

**Step 4:** Macht einen **Zeitplan** für eure Arbeiten, an den sich alle halten.

**Step 5:** Am Ende der Arbeit sollte ein **Rückblick** stehen: Besprecht, was gut war und wo ihr Verbesserungsmöglichkeiten seht.

## 34 Giving feedback ➜ *SB (p. 189)*

Bei deiner Rückmeldung solltest du drei Dinge beachten:

- Halte dich an die Punkte, zu denen du Rückmeldung geben sollst, z. B. die Aussprache und Verständlichkeit bei einem Dialog, die Rechtschreibfehler in einem Text, das Einhalten eines roten Fadens in einer Geschichte usw. Begründe deine Einschätzungen.
- Gib deine Rückmeldung mit Respekt – niemand soll sich angegriffen fühlen. Nenn zuerst Gelungenes und mach dann Verbesserungsvorschläge zu Punkten, die noch nicht so gelungen sind.
- Wenn du selbst eine Rückmeldung bekommst, überdenke die Vorschläge gut. Korrigiere die Fehler, die andere gefunden haben, und arbeite an den Stellen nach, wo du eventuell Probleme hattest.

## 35 Understanding new words ➜ SB (p. 189)

- Viele englische Wörter werden ähnlich wie im Deutschen geschrieben oder klingen ähnlich (z. B. *brochure, statue, insect*). Manche sehen auch einem Wort aus anderen Sprachen ähnlich, z. B. *voice (French: voix; Latin: vox)*.
- In manchen Wörtern stecken bekannte Teile, z. B. *bottle opener, snowshoe*.
- Präfixe und Suffixe wie *un-*, *re-* und *-er* helfen beim Erschließen: *listen**er** (sb. who listens), **un**happy <> happy, **re**pay (pay back)*.
- Bilder zum Text zeigen oft Dinge, die du im Text vielleicht nicht verstehst.
- Der Kontext kann beim Verstehen helfen, z. B. *Let's hurry. The train* ***departs*** *in ten minutes*.

## 36 Using a dictionary ➜ SB (p. 190)

### ZWEISPRACHIGE WÖRTERBÜCHER

Die Leitwörter *(running heads)* oben auf der Seite helfen dir, schnell zu finden, was du suchst. Auf der linken Seite steht das erste Stichwort, auf der rechten Seite das letzte Stichwort der Doppelseite.

- *resign* ist das **Stichwort** *(headword)*. Stichwörter sind alphabetisch geordnet: *r* vor *s*, *ra* vor *re*, *rhe* vor *rhi* usw.
- Die **kursiv gedruckten** Hinweise helfen dir, die für deinen Text passende Bedeutung zu finden.
- Die **Ziffern 1, 2** usw. zeigen, dass ein Stichwort unterschiedliche Bedeutungen haben oder unterschiedlichen Wortarten angehören kann (z. B. Adjektiv, Nomen, Verb).
- **Beispielsätze und Redewendungen** sind dem Stichwort zugeordnet.
- **Unregelmäßige Verbformen**, besondere **Pluralformen**, die **Steigerungsformen der Adjektive** und ähnliche Hinweise stehen oft in Klammern oder sind kursiv gedruckt.
- Die **Lautschrift** gibt Auskunft darüber, wie das Wort ausgesprochen und betont wird.

> **resort**
>
> **resign** /rɪˈzaɪn/
> **1** BERUF • *als Vorsitzender usw* zurücktreten: *He* ***resigned from*** *the company.* Er verließ das Unternehmen.
> **2** *(job, post)* aufgeben *(Stelle, Posten)*
> **3** **resign oneself to something** sich mit etwas abfinden
>
> **resignation** /ˌrezɪɡˈneɪʃn/
> **1** BERUF • *bei Unternehmen* Kündigung; *von Minister usw* Rücktritt
> **2** **hand in one's resignation** *von Angestelltem* kündigen; *von Minister usw* sein Amt niederlegen
> **3** *Gemütszustand* Resignation
>
> **resigned** /rɪˈzaɪnd/ *(look, sigh)* resigniert

### EINSPRACHIGE WÖRTERBÜCHER

Wenn du selbst einen Text schreibst, kannst du ein einsprachiges Wörterbuch zu Hilfe nehmen. Hierin findest du mehr als in einem zweisprachigen Wörterbuch:

- Ein einsprachiges Wörterbuch erklärt die **Bedeutung** eines Worts **auf Englisch**. Da manche Wörter mehrere Bedeutungen haben, ist es wichtig, alle Einträge und Beispielsätze zu einem Wort zu lesen und mit deinem englischen Text zu vergleichen, um die korrekte Bedeutung herauszufinden.
- Das einsprachige Wörterbuch hilft dir, die **passende Verbindung mit anderen Wörtern** zu finden, z. B. mit Verben und Präpositionen oder in bestimmten feststehenden Wendungen. Das ist nützlich, wenn du nach den richtigen Wörtern für deinen englischen Text suchst.

> **deadly** [ˈdedli] *adj*
> **1** *able or likely to kill people* {= lethal}: This is no longer a deadly disease.
> ***deadly to*** The HSN virus is deadly to chickens.
> ***a deadly weapon*** The new generation of biological weapons is more deadly than ever.
> **2** *(only before noun)* {= complete}:
> ***a deadly secret*** Don't tell anyone – this is a deadly secret.
> ***deadly serious*** *completely serious:* Don't laugh – I am deadly serious!
> **3** *(informal) very boring*: Many TV programmes are pretty deadly!

## 37 Using an online translator ➔ *SB (p. 191)*

Für **einzelne Wörter** kannst du *online translators* verwenden – sie funktionieren im Prinzip wie Wörterbücher. Das geht schnell, kann aber auch ein paar Nachteile haben:

- Ein Wörterbuch (online oder als Buch) gibt dir wesentlich mehr Informationen, u. a. Beispielsätze mit dem gesuchten Wort.
- Übersetzungsmaschinen geben dir oft nicht alle korrekten Übersetzungen, sondern nur ein oder zwei Möglichkeiten oder aber die gängigsten.
- Übersetzungsmaschinen bieten dir keinen Kontext, was es schwerer für dich macht, das richtige Wort zu finden.

**Ganze Sätze** oder gar Texte mit Übersetzungsmaschinen vom Deutschen ins Englische zu übertragen, ist keine gute Idee, weil die künstliche Intelligenz, die dahintersteckt, dabei immer noch zu viele Fehler macht. Vor allem bei folgenden Dingen haben Übersetzungsmaschinen Probleme:

- **Grammatik:** Da die Übersetzungsmaschinen von Wörtern ausgehen und nicht von der Satzstruktur, entstehen gerade bei komplexeren Sätzen schnell Fehler.
- **Idiome:** Aus demselben Grund sind auch Idiome und geflügelte Worte ein Problem, denn die Maschine kann die oftmals nicht-wörtliche Bedeutung nicht erkennen.
  Ein Beispiel: „Fällt dir die Decke auf den Kopf?“ kann völlig falsch mit *„Do you get the ceiling on your head?“* wiedergegeben werden.
- **Regionale Sprachbesonderheiten:** Manche Wörter und Ausdrücke sind regionalspezifisch (oder heute weniger gebräuchlich) und werden von *online translators* nicht erkannt, z. B. wenn „Feudel“ mit „Feudel“ statt mit *floor-cloth* übersetzt wird.

## 38 Using the Internet to improve your vocabulary ➔ *SB (p. 192)*

Das Internet bietet dir auch die Möglichkeit, dein Englisch zu verbessern und deinen Wortschatz zu erweitern.

### LESEN UND SCHREIBEN

- Lies regelmäßig Blogs/Webseiten zu Themen, die dich interessieren.
- Lies Nachrichten online, z. B. auf den Seiten von Zeitungen wie dem *Guardian* (GB) oder der *New York Times* (USA).
- Lade dir kostenlose E-Books herunter. Das *Project Gutenberg* hat z. B. eine große Auswahl.
- Starte einen eigenen Blog und/oder kommentiere Artikel in anderen Blogs. Tausche dich so mit anderen Nutzern aus.

### HÖREN UND SEHEN

- Finde Radiostationen online, z. B. *NPR, BBC World Service* oder *Voice of America*, oder suche Podcasts, die dich interessieren.
- Sieh dir regelmäßig Clips und Filme an.
  Seiten wie *YouTube* bieten jede Menge Nachrichtenclips oder auch Dokumentationen.
- Webseiten wie die des *British Council* oder der *BBC* bieten gute Podcasts zum Thema Englisch und Englischlernen.
- Auf Seiten wie *LibriVox* kannst du kostenlose Audiobücher herunterladen und anhören.

### WORTSCHATZ

- Verwende Suchmaschinen als Ergänzung zum Rechtschreibcheck deines Schreibprogramms: Gib ein, was du geschrieben hast, und suche danach. Wenn du kaum Ergebnisse bekommst, solltest du deine Kollokation noch mal checken.
- Wenn du online nach Wörtern und Redemitteln suchst, ist eines der ersten Ergebnisse häufig ein Online-Wörterbuch, in dem du dann weitere Bedeutungen und häufige Kollokationen nachlesen kannst.
- Suchmaschinen versuchen, deine Suche vorherzusagen. Dies kannst du nutzen, um gängige Kollokationen und Wortkorrelationen zu finden. Beispiel: Du gibst *shower* ein und es werden auch *shower curtain, shower heads* und *shower thoughts* aufgelistet.

## 39 Ordering and structuring vocabulary and ideas ➔ *SB (p. 193)*

Einige der Formen, die du nutzen kannst, sind:

- Tabellen (***tables***)
- Diagramme (z. B. ***tree diagrams***)
- Mindmaps

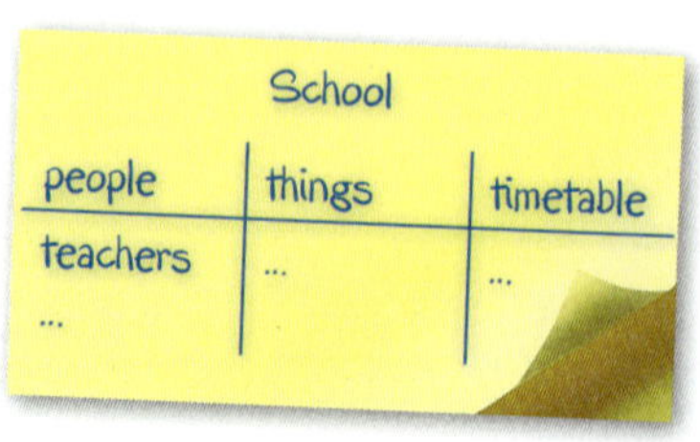


**TIPP:** Wenn du Wortschatz für einen Text zusammenstellst, solltest du daran denken, dass du nicht nur Nomen, sondern auch Verben, Adverbien, Adjektive etc. brauchst, sowie Varianten für Ausdrücke, die häufig vorkommen.

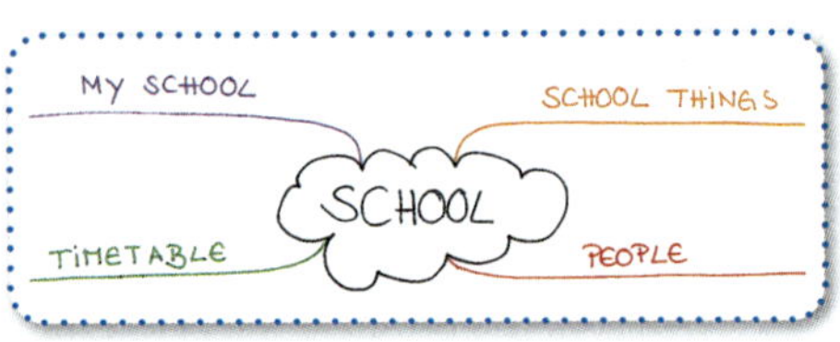


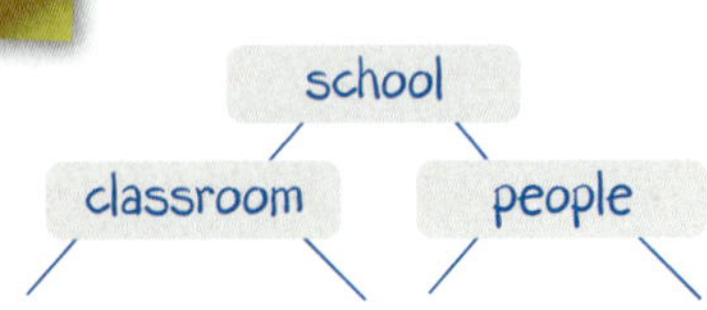

## 40 Working with a grammar ➔ SB (p. 194)

Die Grammatik lernst du im Schulbuch, aber es gibt natürlich auch eigenständige Grammatiken, die du zur Ergänzung nutzen kannst. Der Aufbau einer Grammatik ist dabei meist relativ ähnlich wie die Grammatik in diesem Buch.

**Überschrift**
Hier steht, worum es auf der Seite geht.

**4.4 Das Verb *do*** The verb *do*

**4.4.1 Formen** Forms

Das Verb *do* hat die Formen *do*, *does* (im ***simple present***) und *did* (im ***simple past***).
Die **infiniten Verbformen** (▸ 10.1) lauten:
- *do* (Infinitiv)
- *done* [dʌn] (Partizip Perfekt)
- *doing* (*ing*-Form)

Mit dem Partizip Perfekt *done* bildet man die **Perfektformen** *present perfect (have/has done)*, *past perfect (had done)* und *future perfect (will have done)*.
Mit dem Infinitiv *do* bildet man die **Zukunftsformen** (*will do* und *am/is/are going to do*).

| *simple present* | *simple past* |
|---|---|
| I do | I did |
| you do | you did |
| he does [dʌz] | he did |
| she does | she did |
| it does | it did |
| we do | we did |
| you do | you did |
| they do | they did |

**Zwischenüberschrift**
Wenn ein Thema mehrere Unterthemen hat, gibt es meist entsprechende Unterüberschriften.

**4.4.2 Das Hilfsverb *do*** The auxiliary verb *do*

| | |
|---|---|
| **a** Man verwendet *do/does/did* zur Bildung von **Verneinungen, Fragen, Kurzantworten** und **Frageanhängseln** im *simple present* und *simple past*. | I don't go out very often.<br>What does this word mean?<br>Do you speak English? – Yes, I do.<br>Helen didn't forget your birthday, did she? |
| **b** Man verwendet *don't* (Langform: *do not*) zur **Verneinung des Imperativs**. | Don't go, please.<br>Do not touch. |
| **c** Man kann *do/does/did* verwenden, um das **Vollverb** zu **betonen**.<br>▸ Hervorhebung mit *do*: 1.6.1 | I do ['du:] like the way she bakes her cakes.<br>Do hurry up. |

**Beispiele**
Neben den Erläuterungen (oder darunter) sind Beispiele und Beispielsätze zu finden.

**4.4.3 Das Vollverb *do*** The full verb *do*

| | |
|---|---|
| **a** In der Bedeutung „machen", „tun", „verrichten", „erledigen" ist *do* ein Vollverb. Wie jedes **Tätigkeitsverb** kann es sowohl in der einfachen Form als auch in der Verlaufsform stehen. | Hurricanes do a lot of damage every year.<br>I'm still doing my homework.<br>Next week we're doing lots of activities. |
| **b** **Verneinungen** und **Fragen** im *simple present* und *simple past* bildet man ganz regelmäßig mit *do/does/did*. | We don't usually do much at the weekends.<br>Donald doesn't do much to help his parents.<br>Seth didn't do what his father wanted.<br>When did Jim do his exam? |

**Erklärung/Regeln**
Hier wird das Thema erklärt mit allem, was man dazu beachten muss. Oft gibt es hier auch noch einmal Unterteilungen.

**Auf einen Blick**
- Mit dem **Hilfsverb *do*** bildet man Verneinungen und Fragen: *I **don't** know. / **Do** you know?*
- Auch das **Vollverb *do*** braucht das **Hilfsverb *do***: *I **don't do** crosswords. / **Do** you **do** crosswords?*

**Zusammenfassung**
Oft findet sich am Ende eines Themas oder Unterthemas noch einmal eine Zusammenfassung.

**Weitere Dinge**
Je nach Grammatik und/oder Thema kann es z. B. auch noch nützliche Tipps oder Warnungen vor besonders häufigen Fehlerquellen geben.

## 41 Making and taking notes ➔ SB (p. 195)

Wenn du Informationen oder eigene Gedanken kurz für dich notierst, heißt das im Englischen **making notes**. Wenn du dir Notizen beim Lesen oder Zuhören machst, heißt das **taking notes**. Für beide Varianten gelten aber die gleichen Grundsätze.

**Step 1:** Achte auf **keywords**, um deine Frage/Aufgabe zu beantworten oder den Inhalt eines Textes grob zu verstehen.

**Step 2:** Notiere nur die wichtigsten Informationen. Verwende **Abkürzungen und Symbole**, aber achte darauf, dass du immer dieselben verwendest, damit du deine Notizen später noch verstehst. Markiere offene Fragen.

**Step 3:** Geh im Anschluss an das Lesen oder Hören noch mal durch deine Notizen und ergänze evtl. fehlende Informationen.

**TIPP:** Wenn du kein eigenes System von Abkürzungen hast, kannst du z. B. auch diese verwenden:

| | | | | | | | |
|---|---|---|---|---|---|---|---|
| *the same as* | = | *becomes/will be* | -> | *important* | ! | *open question* | ?? |
| *not the same as* | ≠ | *between* | b/w | *not* | x | | |
| *about the same as* | ≈ | *in other words* | i. e. | *with* | w/ | | |
| *and* | + | *for example* | e. g. | *without* | w/o | | |

## 42 Preparing for a written exam ➜ *SB (pp. 195–197)*

Aufgaben in schriftlichen Tests lassen sich in **geschlossene *(closed)*** und **offene *(open)*Testformate** unterteilen. Es ist bei Klassenarbeiten oder Prüfungen auch möglich, dass es eine Mischung aus geschlossenen und offenen Formaten gibt.

### GESCHLOSSENE AUFGABEN

#### VORBEREITUNG

**Step 1:** Übe die unterschiedlichen Formate wie z. B. **multiple-choice tasks, true/false statements, matching tasks** oder **gapped texts** (Lückentexte), z. B mit dem Klassenarbeitstrainer oder mithilfe dieses SMC. Mache dich mit den verschiedenen Formaten vertraut.

#### DURCHFÜHRUNG

**Step 1:** Lies die Arbeitsanweisungen gut durch. Stelle sicher, dass du genau verstanden hast, was du tun sollst.

**Step 2:** Konzentriere dich auf die Informationen, die du benötigst, um die Aufgaben zu bearbeiten und mache dir Notizen dazu (➜ *SMC 41*).

- Bei **Höraufgaben** versuche so viel wie möglich beim ersten Hören zu verstehen und nutze das zweite Hören, um die Informationen zu vervollständigen. (➜ *SMC 26*)
- Bei **Textaufgaben** lies den Text gründlich (wenn es um Details gehen soll) bzw. skimme/scanne ihn (wenn es um den groben Inhalt geht oder um bestimmte Informationen, (➜ *SMC 1*). Beantworte dann zuerst die Fragen, bei denen du dir sicher bist, und dann die, bei denen du länger nachdenken musst.
- Beantworte immer alle Aufgaben. Wenn du die Antwort nicht weißt, versuche die Antwort zu erschließen.

Hier sind noch einige Tipps, worauf du bei den einzelnen Testformaten besonders achten solltest:

**Multiple-choice tasks**

Bei ***multiple-choice***-Aufgaben sollst du aus mehreren Antwortmöglichkeiten die korrekte auswählen.

- Lies die gegebenen Optionen sehr genau, denn manchmal sind Fallen darin versteckt: sie können z. B Stichwörter aus dem Text enthalten, aber das genaue Gegenteil vom Textinhalt aussagen.
- Wenn du unsicher bist, was die richtige Antwort ist, gehe alle Antwortoptionen durch und überlege, warum sie falsch sein könnten.

**True/false statements**

Bei ***true/false***-Aussagen geht es darum, jede gegebene Aussage hinsichtlich ihres Wahrheitsgehaltes zu überprüfen.

- Um falsche oder wahre Aussagen zu identifizieren, gehe durch den Text und finde Belege dafür. In der Regel kannst du Textstellen finden, die den Inhalt der Aussage widerspiegeln bzw. genau das Gegenteil sagen.
- Manchmal sollst du belegen, weshalb du eine Aussage für wahr oder falsch hältst. Nenne dann Textstellen, die du gefunden hast.

**Matching tasks**

Bei ***matching***-Aufgaben werden Dinge einander zugeordnet, also z. B Absätze und Überschriften oder Satzhälften.

- Ordne Dinge nicht einander zu, nur weil sie sich ähneln oder weil sie Wörter mit ähnlicher Bedeutung enthalten. Zur Sicherheit solltest du den Inhalt für dich umschreiben und nur Dinge mit passendem Inhalt einander zuordnen.

**Gapped texts**

Bei ***gapped texts*** müssen Lücken im Text sinnvoll befüllt werden.

- Achte besonders auf Wörter, die Sätze oder Gedanken verbinden wie z. B ***linking words*** oder Pronomen sowie den Zeitablauf im Text. Diese Stellen können dir gute Hinweise geben, wie Lücken sinnvoll gefüllt werden sollten.
- Wenn du den Text vervollständigt hast, lies ihn nochmal gut durch, um sicher zu stellen, dass die Grammatik passt (Zeiten, Aktiv/Passiv etc.) und dass der Text logisch ist (kausale Zusammenhänge).

### OFFENE AUFGABEN

In den meisten Prüfungen wirst du mit Texten konfrontiert – dies können gedruckte Texte verschiedener **Textsorten** sein, aber auch visuelle Impulse wie Bilder, Cartoons oder Filmclips – oder mit Kombinationen von Texten wie z. B ein Text und ein Bild, zu denen du Aufgaben bearbeiten sollst.

#### VORBEREITUNG

**Step 1:** Erkundige dich, ob Hilfsmittel erlaubt sind (wie z. B Wörterbücher).

**Step 2:** Übe mit alten Prüfungen, um zu sehen, was auf dich zukommen könnte.

**Step 3:** Lerne die wichtigsten Arbeitsanweisungen und was von dir dabei erwartet wird (siehe unten).

**TIPP:** Für die Bearbeitung dieser Aufgaben brauchst du unterschiedliche **Techniken** wie z. B
- ***skimming/scanning*** (➜ *SMC 1*)
- Texte markieren (➜ *SMC 2*)
- Notizen machen (➜ *SMC 41*)

#### DURCHFÜHRUNG

In der Regel werden die Aufgaben zum Text drei Anforderungsbereiche abdecken, zu denen du dich äußern musst. Diese Anforderungsbereiche sind:

- Anforderungsbereich I: Textverständnis
- Anforderungsbereich II: Analyse und Interpretation
- Anforderungsbereich III: Transfer

**TIPP:** Auf diese Dinge solltest du bei den einzelnen Arbeitsaufträgen achten:
- **outline:** Strukturiere deine Antwort in Haupt- und Unterpunkte (➜ *SMC 6*)
- **state:** Sei präzise und erkläre einen oder mehrere Punkte
- **summarize:** Fasse dich kurz und gehe nicht ins Detail (➜ *SMC 13*)

Die unterschiedlichen Anforderungsbereiche haben verschiedene Arbeitsanweisungen, an denen du sie erkennen kannst. Im Folgenden kannst du sehen, was sie bedeuten und was von dir verlangt wird.

**Anforderungsbereich I: Textverständnis**
Diese Aufgaben befassen sich mit dem Inhalt des Textes. Hier sollst du zeigen, dass du den Text verstanden hast. Textverständnisaufgaben können entweder geschlossene Aufgaben oder offene Aufgaben sein.

Im Folgenden findest du Beispiele für typische Aufgaben zur Überprüfung des Textverständnisses. Wichtige Signalwörter für diesen Aufgabenbereich sind **outline, state** sowie **summarize/sum up/write a summary of**.

- Nenne die wichtigsten Punkte oder grundsätzliche Aspekte eines Themas: **Outline the writer's views on ... • Outline/Say why this topic is important.**
- Erläutere einen bestimmten Punkt oder ein bestimmtes Thema im Text: **State the author's opinion on ... •**
- Gib eine knappe Darstellung eines Ereignisses oder Themas im Text oder fasse Inhalte des Textes knapp zusammen: **Summarize the event described in the text. • Sum up the role of person X in this scene. • Write a summary of ...**
- Es kann auch Kombinationen geben: **Summarize the first scene and state why it is important for the rest of the text.**

**Anforderungsbereich II: Analyse/Interpretation**
Bei diesen Aufgaben geht es um ein tieferes Verständnis des Textes. Hier sollst du zeigen, dass du nicht nur den Inhalt, sondern auch die Intention des Autors verstehst. Fragen, die du dir stellen solltest, sind z. B: Warum hat der Autor etwas genau so beschrieben? Was will er/sie damit erreichen? An wen richtet sich der Text? Was sagt die Beschreibung eines Charakters über ihn/sie aus?

Lies die Arbeitsanweisungen genau, damit du weißt, was von dir verlangt wird. Signalwörter für diesen Aufgabenbereich sind **analyse, examine** oder **explain**:

- Beschreibe und erkläre bestimmte Aspekte eines Textes im Detail: **Analyse the main elements of the poster/scene/text.**
- Erläutere einen bestimmten Punkt oder ein bestimmtes Thema im Text: **Examine how the main character is characterised.**
- Beschreibe und definiere ein Ereignis/Thema oder einen bestimmten Punkt im Detail: **Explain the main character's reaction to ...**

> **TIPP:** Auf diese Dinge solltest du bei den einzelnen Arbeitsaufträgen achten:
> - **analyse:** Stelle immer eine Verbindung zwischen verwendeten Stilmitteln und ihrer Wirkung her
> - **examine:** Achte auf das, was im Text konkret steht ebenso wie auf Dinge, die sich "zwischen den Zeilen" befinden.
> - **explain:** Beschreibe nicht nur, sondern begründe anhand des Textes, weshalb Dinge deiner Meinung nach so dargestellt sind, wie sie sind.

**Anforderungsbereich III: Über den Text hinaus**
Aufgaben aus diesem Anforderungsbereich fordern dich oft auf, dich kreativ mit einem Text oder einem Thema auseinanderzusetzen, z. B indem du ein Ende für einen Text oder eine Szene aus der Perspektive eines anderen Charakters schreiben sollst. Hier solltest du darauf achten, dass dein Stil zum Ausgangstext bzw. zu dem Charakter passt. Manchmal ist dir die Textsorte freigestellt, manchmal ist eine bestimmte Textsorte vorgeschrieben.

Beachte auf jeden Fall immer die Grundsätze für das Schreiben guter Texte (➔ *SMC 3 ff.*).

Im Folgenden findest du Beispiele für typische Aufgaben in diesem Anforderungsbereich. Wichtige Signalwörter in den Arbeitsaufträgen sind z. B **comment on, discuss** oder **justify**.

- Gib deine Meinung zu einem Thema und begründe sie mit Belegen aus dem Text: **Comment on the author's belief that ... • Comment on the question of ...**
- Erörtere ein Thema. Bringe dabei Argumente pro und contra ein: **Discuss why it is important for minorities to be represented in films/on TV.**
- Finde Gründe und Belege für deine Meinung/Entscheidung/Schlussfolgerung: **Justify your answer. • Justify why ...**

> **TIPP:** Textsorten, die du in diesem Anforderungsbereich produzieren sollst, können z. B sein:
> - Brief/E-Mail (➔ *SMC 5*)
> - Erörterung (➔ *SMC 7*)
> - Kommentar (➔ *SMC 8*)
> - Leserbrief (➔ *SMC 9*)
> - Artikel (➔ *SMC 10*)
> - Bericht (➔ *SMC 11*)
> - Review (➔ *SMC 12*)

> **TIPP:** Auf diese Dinge solltest du bei den einzelnen Arbeitsaufträgen in der Vorbereitung achten:
> - **comment on:** Bevor du schreibst, sammle Textbelege und strukturiere sie.
> - **discuss:** Wäge beide Seiten des Themas ab und komme zu einer begründeten Schlussfolgerung.
> - **justify:** Markiere Textstellen, die deine Aussage stützen oder begründen.

## 43 Preparing for a speaking exam ➜ *SB (pp. 198–199)*

Auf Sprechprüfungen/Kommunikationsprüfungen kannst du dich ebenso vorbereiten wie auf schriftliche Prüfungen.

### WIE SIEHT DIE PRÜFUNG AUS?

**Step 1:** Als erstes solltest du herausfinden, um welche Art von Prüfung es sich handelt. Es gibt zwei Formen: monologisches Sprechen oder dialogisches Sprechen (oder eine Kombination von beidem, z. B zuerst ein Monolog, gefolgt von einem Dialog zu einem bestimmten Thema).

- **Monologisches Sprechen**
  - Präsentation/Mündlicher Vortrag als Reaktion auf einen Impuls
  - Präsentation/Mündlicher Vortrag zu einem Thema (spontan oder vorbereitet)
- **Dialogisches Sprechen**
  - Gespräch mit einem Lehrer oder der Prüfungskommission
  - Gespräch mit einer/m oder mehreren Partnern/Partnerinnen

**Step 2:** Informiere dich über weitere Aspekte:

- **Partner:** Kannst du eine/n Partner selbst wählen oder wird er/sie zugeteilt? Könnt ihr vor der Prüfung gemeinsam üben?
- **Format:** Welche Form hat die Prüfung? Freies Sprechen zu einem Thema oder bekommst du einen Impuls (Text, Bild etc.)?
- **Dauer:** Wie lange dauert die Prüfung/die einzelnen Teile?
- **Vorbereitung:** Wann erfährst du das Thema? Kannst du dich zu Hause vorbereiten oder erst direkt vor dem Test?
- **Medien:** Sollst du Medien (Computer, Folien etc.) verwenden? Wieviel Zeit hast du, diese vorzubereiten?
- **Benotung:** Wie wird die Prüfung benotet? In der Regel setzt sich die Note aus Inhalt und sprachlicher Kompetenz zusammen.

**Step 3:** Sammle alle Informationen wie z. B auch Musterprüfungen und Informationen zur Benotung in einem Ordner.

### MONOLOGISCHES SPRECHEN

### PRÄSENTATION/MÜNDLICHER VORTRAG ZU EINEM IMPULS

Wenn du in deinem mündlichen Vortrag auf einen Impuls reagieren sollst, kann das z. B ein Bild oder Text sein, aber auch ein Zitat, eine Statistik, ein Cartoon oder eine oder mehrere Fragen. Oft erfährst du das erst kurz vor oder in der Prüfung selbst. Aber auch wenn du nicht genau weißt, mit welcher Art von Impuls du konfrontierst wird, kannst du dich vorbereiten:

- Erstelle eine Mindmap oder Liste für jede Art von möglichem Impuls.
- Sammle darin Wörter oder ganze Sätze, um über die verschiedenen Impulse zu sprechen. Dies hilft dir, deinen Vortrag zu strukturieren, und deinem Gegenüber, ihm zu folgen. Lerne diese Redewendungen – wenn du sie sicher beherrschst, kannst du dich in der Prüfungssituation auf die Inhalte konzentrieren. (➜ *SMC 21, 22, 23, 24*)

### PRÄSENTATION / MÜNDLICHER VORTRAG ZU EINEM THEMA

Wenn du für deine Prüfung eine Präsentation/einen mündlichen Vortrag zu einem Thema vorbereiten sollst, gehe dabei vor wie bei anderen Präsentationen auch (➜ *SMC 29, 30*).

Einige Punkte solltest du aber besonders beachten:

- **Struktur:** Stelle sicher, dass die Zuhörer deiner Präsentation gut folgen können. Lerne und verwende Redewendungen wie *first of all, finally, next.*
- **Medien:** Bereite alle Medien (Bilder, Präsentationen etc.) gut vor. Dazu gehören z. B auch deine Notizen, am besten auf Karteikarten.
- **Zeitmanagement:** Halte dich an die vorgegebene Zeit. Das schaffst du am besten, wenn du deine Präsentation ein paar Mal laut übst, z. B vor einem Partner.
- **Vortrag:** Sieh die Prüfer an, wenn du sprichst, nicht deine Notizen. Sprich langsam, deutlich und lass dir ruhig Zeit, zwischendurch mal tief Luft zu holen, besonders wenn du nervös bist. Mach das auch schon beim Üben.

### DIALOGISCHES SPRECHEN – AN GESPRÄCHEN TEILNEHMEN

Oft beinhaltet eine mündliche Prüfung auch einen dialogischen Teil, in dem du mit einem Partner oder den Prüfern kommunizierst.

Dies kann z. B ein Gespräch zu einem Thema sein, aber auch eine Diskussion, ein Interview oder ein Rollenspiel. Auch wenn du nicht genau weißt, mit was du in der Prüfung konfrontierst wird, kannst du dich auf die Situation vorbereiten.

**Step 1:** Überlege dir, evtl. mit einem Partner/einer Partnerin, im Vorfeld für jede der möglichen Formen – Gespräch, Diskussion, Interview, Rollenspiel – worauf du dabei achten musst.

**Step 2:** Notiere dir, was du an Phrasen und Redewendungen für die einzelnen Phasen eines Dialoges brauchst und lerne sie. (➜ *SMC 22*)

- Anfang einer Diskussion: **Today we're talking about … • Let me start with … • …**
- Zustimmen/widersprechen: **What a great / … idea. • My point exactly. • … / That's not how I see it. • I don't agree with …**
- Nachfragen: **Can you give an example of that? • Do you mean …?**
- Eine/n Partner/in einbeziehen: **How about you? • What do you think / How do you feel about that?**
- Unterbrechen: **May I interrupt? • Excuse me, can I just say that …?**
- Zeit zum Überlegen gewinnen: **Can I repeat what we said before? • Well, now let me see … • Let me think about that for a second.**
- Zusammenfassen: **We've seen that … • To come to a conclusion …**

**TIPP:** Beachte auch diese allgemeinen Tipps für die Prüfungssituation:
- Erstelle deine Notizen so, dass du sie schnell finden und auf einen Blick entziffern kannst.
- Sei gut ausgeschlafen. Trage angemessene Kleidung, in der du dich auch wohlfühlst. Sei pünktlich.
- Sei höflich und freundlich. Bedenke auch, dass du in einer dialogischen Prüfungssituation nicht für deine eigene Note arbeitest, sondern auch für deine/n Partner/in.

## 44 Preparing for a listening exam ➜ *SB (pp. 200–201)*

Auf Hörverstehensprüfungen kannst du dich ebenso vorbereiten wie auf schriftliche oder mündliche Prüfungen.

### WAS WIRD GEPRÜFT?

Ein *listening exam* überprüft deine Hörverstehenskompetenz.
Dabei sollst du zeigen, dass du
- Gesprächen folgen kannst,
- Gesprächen und längeren Hörtexten Hauptpunkte und wichtige Details entnehmen kannst *(gist and detail)*,
- die wesentlichen Einstellungen der Sprechenden identifizieren kannst, also z. B. sagen kannst, wie jemand auf etwas reagiert, das im Hörtext passiert.

### WIE SIEHT DIE PRÜFUNG AUS?

Du wirst in einer Prüfung zwei Arten von Aufgaben begegnen: geschlossenen Aufgaben und halboffenen Aufgaben. Meist wird deine Prüfung aus einer Mischung aus beidem bestehen.

| Geschlossene Aufgaben | Halboffene Aufgaben |
|---|---|
| ↓ | ↓ |
| Multiple Choice<br>Matching | Fill in<br>Short answers |

Beispiele für die vier Aufgabenformate findest du auf der nächsten Seite.

### VORBEREITUNG

Hier sind einige Dinge, die du im Vorfeld der Prüfung zur Vorbereitung klären kannst:
- **Dauer:** Besteht die Prüfung aus mehreren Teilen? Wenn ja, wieviele Teile sind es? Wie lange dauert die Prüfung/die einzelnen Teile?
- **Format:** Sieh dir die möglichen Aufgabenformate an und mache dich mit ihnen vertraut.
- **Benotung:** Wie wird die Prüfung benotet? Haben die unterschiedlichen Aufgabenformate in der Prüfung eine unterschiedliche Gewichtung?

### DURCHFÜHRUNG

- Lies die Arbeitsanweisungen gut durch, am besten vor dem ersten Hören. Stelle sicher, dass du genau verstanden hast, was du tun sollst.
- Konzentriere dich auf die Informationen, die du benötigst, um die Aufgaben zu bearbeiten und mache dir kurze, stichwortartige Notizen dazu (➔ *SMC41*).
- Versuche so viel wie möglich beim ersten Hören zu verstehen und nutze das zweite Hören, um deine Informationen zu vervollständigen. (➔ *SMC26*)
- Beantworte immer alle Aufgaben. Wenn du die Antwort nicht weißt, versuche die Antwort zu erschließen.

### AUFGABENFORMATE

Generell können alle genannten Formate alle Aspekte des Hörverstehens überprüfen (*gist, detail*, Einstellungen der Sprechenden). Im Folgenden findest du ein paar Beispielaufgaben, damit du ein Gespür dafür bekommst, welche Fragestellung auf welche Informationen abzielt.

#### Multiple Choice

Multiple Choice-Aufgaben bestehen in der Regel aus einer Frage oder Aussage sowie mehreren Möglichkeiten, die Frage zu beantworten bzw. die Aussage zu vervollständigen.

**1** Peter talks to Fred about …
a) his hobbies.
b) Fred's hobbies.
c) his dad's hobbies.

**2** How does Fred react to Peter's plans?
a) He is surprised.
b) He is angry.
c) He is confused.

Beispiel 1 überprüft, ob du spezifische Details korrekt heraushören kannst (über wessen Hobbies wird gesprochen?). Beispiel 2 überprüft, ob du Aussagen im Zusammenhang erfassen kannst (Kannst du aus dem Gesagten erschließen, was der Sprecher/die Sprecherin denkt/meint/fühlt?).

#### Matching

Bei Matching-Aufgaben musst du Dinge einander zuordnen.

**Who says what?**

| | |
|---|---|
| 1 Jack | a) thinks climate change isn't a problem at all. |
| 2 Peter | b) thinks climate change is a problem but not a big one. |
| 3 Fred | c) thinks climate change is a really big problem. |
| 4 Simon | d) thinks climate change is the biggest problem we have today. |

Bei diesem Beispiel oben sollst du aus dem Gesagten heraushören, was die Sprecher genau sagen/meinen.

#### Fill in

Bei diesem Format sollst du Infomationen mithilfe des Hörtextes ergänzen.

People in New York City are afraid that ______________________________.

Dieses Beispiel überprüft, ob du spezifische Details korrekt heraushören kannst.

#### Short answers

Bei diesem Format musst du Fragen beantworten. Hier hilft es, wenn du dir beim Hören Notizen gemacht hast.

Why do many people think that New York is the most exciting city in the world?

______________________________________________.

Dieses Beispiel überprüft, ob du die Gesamtaussage des Textes verstanden hast.

## 1 A visit to Rotorua City and the Māori village of Whakarewarewa

You are on a visit to the Māori village of Whakarewarewa. During your visit you listen to an audio guide. First read the tasks. You have 90 seconds to do this. Then listen to the audio guide and do the tasks. At the end you will hear the audio guide again and you can check your answers.

1 The ancestors of the villagers arrived in the area over …

A ☐ 1000 years ago.

B ☐ 700 years ago.

C ☐ 7000 years ago.

2 The villagers decided to open their home to strangers

______________________________.

3 In the meeting house, you can learn about Māori history by …

A ☐ reading written legends.

B ☐ listening to speeches.

C ☐ looking at wooden pictures.

4 The local Māori can ______________________

______________________ which is heated by underground volcanic activity.

5 Visitors should know that the tour to Te Rata Bay goes over …

A ☐ rough ground. B ☐ narrow stairs.

C ☐ a high bridge.

6 The Pāhutu Geyser erupts …

A ☐ once a day. B ☐ every six hours.

C ☐ many times a day.

7 In Māori culture, hāngī is a traditional ______________

______________________________.

8 Do this task **after** you have listened to the whole guided tour. Which statement best describes the **whole tour**?

A ☐ A presentation of multicultural New Zealand.

B ☐ A presentation of traditional life in modern times.

C ☐ A presentation of a way of life that has disappeared.

## 2 Pata Café, Christchurch

As part of a class project about running your own business, you come across a radio interview between the host, Paul Rutherford, and Moana Parata, owner of the Pata Café in Christchurch, New Zealand. First read the tasks. You have 90 seconds to do this. Then listen to the interview and do the tasks. At the end you will hear the interview again and you can check your answers.

1 The host, Paul, is talking to someone who …

A ☐ lost her café in the earthquake.

B ☐ didn't let the earthquake destroy her project.

C ☐ began a new project after the earthquake.

2 Due to the earthquake, the tribe's ______________ were destroyed.

3 In her work, Moana became aware of the fact that …

A ☐ modern farming was dangerous.

B ☐ Māori traditions could disappear.

C ☐ her tribe loved farming.

4 Moana's business is not just a simple café because

________ also ______________________.

5 According to Māori tradition, there are rules around

______________________________

______________________________.

6 Moana hopes that her café …

A ☐ benefits her tribe. B ☐ makes money.

C ☐ can employ more workers.

7 On the day of the visit, the café is ______________.

8 Do this task **after** you have listened to the whole interview. Which motto best fits Moana's café project?

A ☐ Good for your Pocket and your Stomach.

B ☐ Taste the Māori Legacy.

C ☐ Māori Food for Body and Mind.

## 3 Taika Waititi

**As part of a project in your English class on English-language movies, you want to present a star of superhero movies to your class. You have come across the Māori movie writer, director and actor, Taika Waititi. Find out more about him in the online article.**

"I think comedy is very important because it helps us deal with things that are difficult or painful." So says Taika Waititi, one of the most famous – and successful - New Zealanders on the planet right now.
Waititi is probably best known as the director of movies such as *JoJo Rabbit* (2019) and two of Marvel's *Thor* superhero movies, with more in the pipeline.
His belief in comedy as a way of dealing with life's challenges might come from his childhood: born in 1975 in Raukokore on New Zealand's North Island, the young Waititi grew up in a mixed-race family. His father is a Māori artist and his mother a schoolteacher of Jewish, Irish, Scottish and English descent. However, Waititi's parents divorced when he was just five years old and at times his mother had to work three jobs to support them.
Waititi's first steps in comedy and acting began in high school in Wellington and he went on to study drama at university. His early career involved a period as a stand-up comedian and stage actor as well as minor roles in TV series and movies. But Waititi realised early on that his real desire was to tell his own stories from behind, not in front of, the camera. This stage of his career could not have had a better start when his first short movie, *Two Cars, One Night*, starring a mainly Māori cast, was nominated in 2005 for an Oscar. He lost out on that occasion to British filmmaker Andrea Arnold. He completed his first full-length movie, *Eagle Vs. Shark*, a romantic comedy, two years later. His next movie, *Boy* (2010) became the most financially successful New Zealand movie ever. The movie was based on Waititi's childhood experiences and featured his own father's artwork.
Black humour and sharp, witty dialogue have been constant features of Waititi's work and the influence of New Zealand and Māori heritage is never far away. One of his first movies to earn international commercial success was *What We do in the Shadows* (2014), a mock documentary following the lives of a group of vampires living in modern-day Wellington. The moviemaker's sense of fun on the set and his comedy talents brought him to the attention of Marvel Studios and they asked him to reimagine Thor the Viking superhero in two of their movies, *Thor: Ragnorok* (2017) and *Thor: Love and Thunder* (2022). Although working for one of Hollywood's biggest studios, Waititi didn't forget his roots: he made sure the studio allowed Indigenous trainees to gain experience in all aspects of the movies' production.
While the Marvel films have brought Waititi the most commercial success so far, it was 2020 which saw Waititi win the movie business's highest award. *JoJo Rabbit*, his movie adaptation of the of the book *Caged Skies* earned Waititi an Oscar for best screenplay. The original story of a ten-year-old Hitler Youth member in wartime Germany did not contain as much comedy as the movie does and it certainly did not feature the boy's imaginary friend – a bumbling Adolf Hitler (played by Waititi himself) – but after meeting Waititi, the book's Kiwi author, Christine Leunens, had no reservations about him changing the story in his distinctive style. She believes it is Waititi's Māori background which enables him to deal with the joy and sadness of life in a way that touches people and makes them both laugh and cry.

**Tick (✓) the correct box or complete the sentences. For true/false and multiple-choice questions, write evidence for your answer in your exercise book.**

1 Taika Waititi has stopped making movies.

This statement is ☐ true ☐ false.

2 When Waititi was young, his family experienced …

**A** ☐ an accident. **B** ☐ health problems. **C** ☐ poverty.

3 After a short time acting, Waititi discovered his true wish was to make films, not act in them.

This statement is ☐ true ☐ false.

4 Waititi's work as a filmmaker began very successfully when he almost ______________________.

5 Waititi tries to use his success to help other people with a similar cultural background.

This statement is ☐ true ☐ false.

6 Superhero movies have earned Waititi the most …

**A** ☐ awards. **B** ☐ money. **C** ☐ praise.

7 *JoJo Rabbit* was ______________________ the original novel *Caged Skies*.

## 4 Education in the UK for over-16s

As you will begin *Oberstufe* next year, your English teacher shares some information with the class on the education system in Britain for over-16s. Fill in suitable words or underline the correct words.

1 Sixteen-year-olds in the UK **make / write / do / stand** state exams at the end of year 11. In England, Wales and Northern Ireland, these are the GCSEs (General Certificate of Secondary Education) and in Scotland they are called the Nationals.

2 Studies for GCSE exams take place **by / over / through / between** a period of two or three academic years, starting in Year 9 or Year 10.

3 British young people may leave *school* at 16, but *education* is ______________ up to the age of eighteen so school-leavers must find some form of training if they do decide to stop schooling.

4 Many English students over 16 go on to study for their A (Advanced) or AS (Advanced Subsidiary) Levels. An A Level course **spends / lasts / follows / ends** two years and involves studying one subject with a written exam at the end. The AS Level courses are shorter with exams after one year's study.

5 Although the maximum number of A Levels a student can take is five, only a tiny fraction of students (0.1 % in 2019) do this – the ______________ (61.8 % in 2019) take three A Levels.

6 In 2021, more students did A Levels in Maths than in any other subject and in 2022 Maths remained most ______________, accounting for 11.3 % of all entries at A Level.

7 The two years in which students study for A Levels are called sixth form in England. Most students change schools to **participate / do / visit / attend** sixth form colleges, but some comprehensive schools have separate sixth form facilities and students there can simply remain in their old school.

8 A and AS Level results are an important part of the application process to British universities. This process is ______________ by a central system called UCAS.

9 Using the UCAS system, a student can ______________ up to five universities for a place.

10 The application process normally begins in the October of the students' final sixth form year so, as well as a personal statement, the applications include predictions from teachers about what final grades students are ______________ achieve in their A Levels.

11 For some universities (such as Oxford or Cambridge) and some courses, applicants also have to **take part in / take place in / carry out / conduct** interviews and their performance can form part of the university's decision whether to offer a place or not.

12 When it comes to offering places, universities can make unconditional offers (the offer is guaranteed) or conditional offers (the offer ______________ the actual final grades).

13 Successful applicants may accept their offer of a place but defer – up to ten percent of British students wait a year before **begin / beginning / choose / delaying** their studies.

14 Applicants who defer often use this year, commonly known as a 'gap year', to ______________ experience working, volunteering and/or travelling.

## 5 Frances' Cambridge Interview: extract from *Radio Silence* by Alice Oseman

Frances Janvier is a 17-year-old British mixed-race girl. Always a high-achiever at school, everyone expects her to go on to study at Cambridge University after her A-Level exams. As part of her application to Cambridge, she takes part in an interview at the university.

I messaged Mum that I was going in and she messaged back saying she believed in me. I just wished I believed in me, to be honest. [...]
The two interviewers were both old white men. I'm sure that not all of the interviewers at the University of Cambridge are old white men, and in my second interview later that day one of them was a woman, but in my first interview, mine were old white men, and I was not surprised. They didn't offer to shake my hand, so I didn't offer either. My interview went a little bit like this.

**Old White Man (O.W.M.) #1:** So, Frances, I see that you picked art A level alongside English, history and politics. And you did maths at AS level. Why such a diverse group of subjects?
**Frances:** Oh ... well, you know, I've always been interested in a wide range of subjects. I just thought, at A level, you know, it'd be good to, sort of, keep that going, using both sides of the brain, having a wider ... broader ... learning experience. I enjoy lots of different subjects, so, yeah.
**O.W.M. #1:** *[blinks and nods]*
**O.W.M. #2:** And you say in your personal statement that the book that really started your interest in the study of English literature was *[glances at paper] The Catcher in the Rye* by J. D. Salinger?
**Frances:** Yes!
**O.W.M. #2:** What was it, precisely, about the book that so inspired you?
**Frances:** *[completely unprepared for a question like this]* Ah ... yeah. Well, I think it was the themes, really, I really related to the themes of, you know, disillusionment and alienation, *[laughs]* you know, the typical teenage thing you go through! Erm, but yeah, there were lots of things in the book that really interested me from, like, an academic point of view, like, erm ... One of the things I liked was the way Salinger sort of got the lingo of nineteen-forties and -fifties teenagers? It was the first time I'd read an old book – well, like, a classic book anyway – that, erm, you know, really felt like it had a real voice? I really felt connected to the main character, I guess ... and it made me want to understand why.
**O.W.M. #2:** *[nods and smiles, but doesn't really seem to have heard anything I've just said]*
**O.W.M. #1:** So, Frances, I suppose the big question is: why do you want to study English literature?
**Frances:** *[horrific pause]* Well ... *[another horrific pause – why couldn't I think of anything to say?]* Well, I-I've always loved English literature. *[A third horrific pause. Come on. There are more reasons than that. It's fine. Take your time.]* English literature has always been my favourite subject. *[That's not true, is it?]* I've been passionate about studying it at university since I was little. *[What absolute bullshit. You're going to have to sound less like a robot if you want them to believe you.]* I love analysing texts and learning about their— their contexts. *[I don't understand, why are you being like this? You sound like you're lying.]* I think doing an English literature degree would encourage me to read a lot more than I do. *[Wait, so you're saying you don't read lots already? Why are you applying to study English literature in the first place?]* I think ... *[Why are you applying to study English literature at university?]* I think I've always ... *[Always what? Always been lying to yourself about this? Always believed that you were passionate about something you weren't?]*
**O.W.M. #2:** Okay, well, let's move on.

a) Describe how well Frances has prepared for her interview.

b) Analyse how the change in Frances' feelings is shown in the text. To do this, look at how the story is told (narrative technique, use of language).

c) Here you can choose between two different options. Do only **one** of them!

1 Imagine you are Frances. You arrive home after your interviews and talk to your mother.
**Write** the dialogue. Include the following aspects:
- your performance at the interviews
- your feelings about your future
- your mother's reaction

2 A subtitle of Alice Oseman's novel *Radio Silence* is "Listen to your own voice".
**Comment** on the importance of this statement for young people today. Include the following aspects:
- what the statement means to you
- the influence of adults such as parents, teachers, etc. on you
- the influence of friends, peers, etc. on you

## Checkpoint 1

### 1 WORDS A profile

2 huge 3 absolutely 4 fairly 5 particularly 6 conventional 7 quite 8 influenced 9 extremely 10 ambitious 11 lot 12 very 13 passionate 14 great 15 musical 16 not 17 especially

### 2 Why is he being photographed?

2 Why are the scientists being arrested? 3 Why is her car being stopped? 4 Where is the device being taken? 5 Why is that woman being watched? 6 How is the information being sent?

### 3 Writing an opinion piece: language structures

a) 1 ✔ 3 ✔

b) 1 mustn't 2 ought to 3 should 4 can 5 has to 6 must

### 4 Writing an opinion piece: tips for Maddison

- You should make the first paragraph short.
- State your opinion and topic clearly in the first paragraph.
- You should use things like quotes and statistics to back up your main statement.
- Include the personal pronouns **I**, **you** and **we**: e.g., **I** shows how strongly you feel.
- Tell anecdotes about things that have happened to you.
- Use less well-known facts to surprise your reader.
- Use rhetorical questions to say things in a more emphatic way.
- Let me read it when you have finished!

### 5 Money and identity: writing an opinion piece

a) **Follow the guidelines for writing an opinion piece. Ideas:**
- being afraid of not having enough money or losing it
- not having enough money → being afraid of living in need, thinking: more money can change the situation → influence our thoughts/identity
- not spending a lot: (1) positive: people don't focus on material things; (2) negative: people see themselves and others as losers
- spending/not spending money: influences our emotions → success? failing?
- Are my personal strengths connected to money?

b) **Ideas:**
- advertisements: everywhere (on TV, online, at the cinema, in magazines, on the street, in shop windows), big business
- the newest object: we = happy, the 'right' kind of life → wrong
- our value as people ≠ the things we own
- Jonathan Swift: A wise person should have money in their head, but not in their heart.
- adverts
  - influence us: the problem is that we want the things we see in adverts and we feel bad if we don't get them
  - appeal to our emotions instead of using facts
- some people: afraid of being laughed at if they don't have the latest clothes → importance of money, shopping, technical devices, etc.
- attack our self-confidence → our identity is linked to what we can and cannot buy
- extremely difficult situation for young people who are trying to find their place in the world
- solution: limit the number of adverts by law, don't allow companies to make any adverts for children
- better: focus on human beings and relationships

## Checkpoint 2

### 1 We do need to take action

1 Young people do need to start campaigning.
It's young people who need to start campaigning.
Young people need to start campaigning themselves.
Young people definitely need to start campaigning.

2 My MP does get involved in local projects.
It's my MP who gets involved in local projects / It's local projects that my MP gets involved in.
My MP gets involved in local projects herself/himself.
My MP really gets involved in local projects.

### 2 *Boxes of Hope*: a community project

1 of feeling 2 of doing 3 of starting 4 in being 5 on receiving 6 of making 7 in giving 8 of bringing

### 3 The European Parliament in Brussels

a) **Text 1:** include plenaries and committee meetings
**Text 3:** the European Parliament's visitor centre / in the Parliament's Espace Leopold complex in Brussels / There's no need to book

b) 1 **Text 1:** you can watch all public events online/streaming
2 **Text 3:** Visits don't cost a cent

### 4 *Step Inside*: helping people back ...

a) 1 The clothes sold in the shop are different because they are used. 2 It was a good idea to start a shop because people often give clothes to the organization, but the organization can't use everything. 3 The location is a nice area with lovely shops. 4 The students who helped Phil took photos, then they were allowed to use the photos for their college design project, and they got very good marks. 5 This year, the charity has helped nearly 800 people to get a job again. 6 People in the area like the shop because they can take clothes there and know that they are helping the charity.

b) *l. 1:* boutique – Boutique *l. 4:* brainchild – Idee, Einfall *l. 6:* to sleep rough – im Freien übernachten (obdachlos sein) *l. 8:* donation – Spende *l. 9:* item – Artikel, Gegenstand *l. 16:* marvellous – großartig, wunderbar *l. 19:* customer – Kunde/Kundin *l. 21:* to benefit – profitieren *l. 28:* to invest – investieren

c) **Step Inside:** sells used clothes / team of volunteers / money that they make → *The Dale Centre* / organization: gives homeless people somewhere to sleep in the winter / helps them to find work and a place to live / some: work in the shop to get experience / get clothes from the shop for job interviews / successful project

d) I would buy used clothes from this shop or a similar one: good idea, using old clothes again → good for the environment / cheaper than buying new clothes all the time

## Checkpoint 3

### 1 PRONUNCIATION Word stress

1 alternative 2 battery 3 complex 4 controversial
5 digital 6 electricity 7 exclusive 8 an export
9 to export 10 parasite 11 radioactive 12 vision

### 2 WORDS Defining words

a) 2 to hesitate 3 to charge 4 to replace

b) 2 to bring something to someone's house 3 to relax
4 to know what's going to happen

### 3 Using adverbs

2 New species mean that we can use resources more economically. 3 Luckily the patient recovered completely. 4 We only vaguely understand the threat this issue might cause. 5 Could you please explain concisely what the issue is exactly? 6 I sincerely hope we can come to an agreement on this matter.

### 4 Presenting your opinion in a panel discussion

a) 2 You can't just say that without giving an explanation.
3 I think this is the best idea to proceed. / the problem isn't just going to go away. / this needs to be done immediately.
4 In my opinion, this is the best idea to proceed. / the problem isn't just going to go away. / this needs to be done immediately.
5 I don't think we've got any new ideas. 6 As we have seen, this is the best idea to proceed. / the problem isn't just going to go away. / this needs to be done immediately.

b) 2 I don't think so. The problem is that the plastic will never go away. 3 I agree, the sea is huge, but we are filling it with rubbish. 4 In my opinion, plastic is just as dangerous as radioactive waste. 5 I don't think it's that easy, because it just stays in the water in tiny pieces. 6 You can't say it won't affect your children. It already does.

c) – be well-prepared
– write down your own arguments and think about what arguments the others might present
– present a short statement at the beginning
– remember to listen to others

**Ideas:**
– water pollution: kills fish and kills us
– controlling air pollution for years, but what have we been doing with water?
– filling it more and more with our rubbish: plastic shopping bags
– plastic bags don't just 'disappear'
– US Ocean Service: huge regions with plastic forming a kind of soup
– birds and fish eat that 'soup' → animals: dying
– lots of them = our food
– beaches covered in tins, plastic bags, etc.
– Who wants to go on holiday and swim in a sea full of rubbish?
– worse: soup will not go away
– stop throwing plastic in the sea → the plastic that is there will not disappear → clean it up → not simple
– plans to clean sea
– governments: need to work together, help keep our seas safe for the future
– Keeping our planet clean starts with us, at home.
– think before you want to buy something with lots of plastic
– recycle, reuse glass bottles → better for the environment
– We've only got one planet.